Mediterranea

A Vibrant Culinary Journey Through
Southern Europe, North Africa, and the
Eastern Mediterranean

Hanady Nabut
Creator of Hanady Kitchen

PAGE STREET
PUBLISHING CO.

First published in 2022 by

Page Street Publishing Co.

27 Congress Street, Suite 1511

Salem, MA 01970

www.pagestreetpublishing.com

Distributed by Macmillan, sales in Canada by The Canadian Manda Group.

26   25   24   23   22   1   2   3   4   5

ISBN-13: 978-1-64567-548-8

ISBN-10: 1-64567-548-3

Library of Congress Control Number: 2021937904

Cover and book design by Kylie Alexander for Page Street Publishing Co.

Photography by Hanady Nabut

Printed and bound in the United States

To Salma and Ghaith,
my sources of light and inspiration.

As travelers, we become more detail-oriented. Food becomes more delicious, time more precious, people more interesting, and landscapes more beautiful. Let us be travelers even when we are not traveling.

Table of Contents

Introduction

Coming from a mixed background, I never felt quite at home anywhere. I often felt a deep longing for a home that did not exist. As I grew older, so did my appreciation for being of dual heritage. The kitchen became a place where I could make sense of the world. It was a playground that allowed me to learn the importance of breaking the rules and letting creativity flourish. It was and still is a joyful place where I can connect to my roots in an instant.

Throughout my life, my pantry consisted of ingredients such as sazón, sofrito, guava, tahini, za'atar, and halva. I have vivid childhood memories of my earliest culinary experiences. My Palestinian grandfather, Khaled, taught me to eat pita wraps filled with goat cheese, olive oil, and fresh grapes or figs. And my Spanish grandfather, Antonio, taught me how to eat guava or membrillo with queso fresco. My Puerto Rican grandmother, Anna, taught me the importance of gusto in cooking, especially when she made sofrito. She would say that without it, food had no flavor. To her, *gusto* meant two things: pleasure and taste. The latter meaning has no English equivalent but can be interpreted as the oomph that makes food great. Meanwhile, my Palestinian grandmother, Nema, could not bake without singing traditional folk songs. There was always an element of love and passion intertwined with the act of cooking, because the way that you *feel* about cooking shapes how the food will taste. Gusto results only from doing things with care, attention, and, most importantly, plenty of love. This kind of soul cooking simply cannot be learned in schools. It comes from within and from a connection with food that transcends technicalities. I often connect the dots from the Spanish side of the Mediterranean to the Levantine side, celebrating the similarities across cultures. Food is such a powerful force in bringing people together. And it is most fulfilling when it means something special to those sharing it.

This is the concept of *Mediterranea*. The Mediterranean lifestyle is focused on living and eating well, sharing, and enjoying life. The recipes in this book reflect the flavors that I grew up with and learned to love, the flavors of the lands that surround the Mediterranean Sea. Each country in the region is unique and diverse but tied by common threads. A shared ocean and shared agriculture are just a few. These countries share the qualities of having high-spirited festive traditions and a strong emphasis on community and hospitality. Eating fresh, local, and seasonal ingredients is a way of life. Olives, figs, pomegranates, dates, pumpkins, lemons, oranges, and grapes are all staples in the countries along the Mediterranean coast.

The Mediterranean lifestyle is festive, vibrant, bursting with flavor, and people focused. Yes, eating with good company is part of the Mediterranean diet as well. Cooking and eating slowly, with gusto, with love, and with joy are equally important. Time is always made for enjoying the simple things. People immerse their selves in nature, live active lives, and eat well. Value is placed on respecting food. Produce is enjoyed in its season. Livestock are to live happy and healthy lives. Spices are freshly ground. Cheeses, yogurts, and pickled vegetables are locally made. Even though full-on supermarkets now exist throughout the region, most people still prefer to buy each food group from specialty shops. I used to visit over five shops every time I went out for groceries: the produce market, the butcher shop, the fishmonger's, the bakery, the spice market, and the deli. Each took massive pride in their work, providing only the very best of ingredients. Having lived in the eastern Mediterranean for half a decade, I learned to cook with the seasons. The lack of variety with regard to processed foods also taught me to cook from scratch, ground to plate. I learned that it not only resulted in more nutritious food, but was also so much more delicious. Mediterranean food is focused on seasonal eating. A diverse variety of herbs, wild greens, spinach, and stone fruit in the spring. Grapes, figs, and melon in the summer. Olives, almonds, and pumpkin in the fall. Bright aromatic citrus in the winter. Dishes are often centered on ancient grains such as freekeh, wheat berries, barley, bulgur, and durum wheat, sometimes prepared as semolina, couscous, or maftoul. Pulses such as garbanzo beans, fava beans, lentils, and green beans are staples. Popular meats are lamb, chicken, beef, and game birds such as pigeon or quail. Fish and seafood include sea bass, sea bream, hake, mackerel, monkfish, shrimp, squid, clams, mussels, mullet, sardines, anchovies, and cod.

In this book you will find my interpretations of the flavors that I grew up with. From Southern Spain to the eastern Mediterranean and the Fertile Crescent, from the lands spanning the Great Sea, this book brings together the flavors of the region for a vibrant culinary journey. You will find dishes that feed the souls of vegetarians and carnivores alike, soul food to satisfy our nomadic spirits, and most importantly, food that is made to be shared and to bring people together.

Even though I cannot serve these dishes to you personally, I can give you the method to re-create the same experience at home. And in that way, we bond through the same flavors. We leave our normal lives just for a moment to embrace someone else's world. Whether you are an expat in a foreign land or you found a place where you call home, rest assured the kitchen will also be your preferred place to find comfort and familiarity.

Here's to sharing a plate together and creating vibrant relationships along the way.

With love,

Hanady ♡

Background

I didn't go to culinary school, not formally at least. My culinary training began when I was a child. Growing up in a multicultural family meant being exposed to an abundance of flavors and influences. Before the age of 10, I was improvising and experimenting with the world of condiments that filled my pantry.

My training came also from traveling and living throughout the eastern Mediterranean. Observing the similarities in flavors and cooking techniques within the region was enlightening. I learned how to understand dough by instinct from grandmothers who treated me as their own. I learned the importance of using all of the senses—smell, vision, taste, hearing, and touch—to identify quality spices and produce. Looking deeper into the origins of a culture's cuisine allows us to empathize and truly connect with that cuisine and the people it comes from. When we understand how it came to be and how ingredients evolved, we ultimately learn to cook more freely, without the need for recipes. We cook from the soul.

My greatest lesson of all, however, was cooking in a land where resources and ingredients were scarce. I learned to work with limited supplies. I grew accustomed to using olive oil for foods that would call for butter, or tahini and yogurt in place of cream, or freshly squeezed fruit juice reductions in place of syrups, or ancient grains in place of modern processed ones. I used fruits and vegetables within their seasons because most produce was local. Almost everything was made from scratch because shortcuts simply were not anywhere near available. This taught me creativity, which goes to say that scarcity truly is the basis for invention. When I craved the foods from back home, be it Latin American or from the multitude of cuisines enjoyed in America, I would have to re-create them with ingredients and methods that were accessible. They became my own and filled me with a nostalgia that I never imagined.

I realized that food simply tasted better this way. Whole foods, fresh produce, and seasonal flavors all characterize this lifestyle. This is the Mediterranean way. And more importantly, this is the instinctive human way.

For the Love of Olive Oil

Olive oil is almost sacred throughout the Mediterranean. And if there is one thing that connects the countries of the region, it is the growth of the olive tree. For many families that produce it, olive oil is both livelihood and sustenance. The olive harvest takes place in October in the eastern Mediterranean, and it is the most enchanting time of the year. It represents fruitfulness and abundance, hope and new beginnings, and selflessness and giving.

Olive oil flavors range from fruity to piquant to deep and buttery depending on when the olives are harvested. In Palestine and many parts of the Levant, there is a spicy variety of olive oil that is extracted at the very beginning of fall while the olives are still young. It is the greenest shade of green you will ever see in oil. This olive oil is vibrant, bold, and peppery, tickling your throat as you swallow it. But it is only made in small quantities, as olives release little juice in the early stages of harvest. Later yields tend to produce more oil with softer and more buttery notes. The color of this oil will also be lighter, a pale green or deep golden.

I tend to use a rich and fruity variety of olive oil for everyday cooking. Taste different kinds and see which one you have a preference for. Milder flavors are best for cooking, while fruity, peppery, and piquant oils stand out drizzled over foods.

Having lived in the Mediterranean, I acquired the habit of using olive oil for most recipes, even sweets and cakes. Olive oil not only contributes a deep flavor but also makes for a moister crumb in comparison to butter. The pumpkin, olive oil, and almond cake (page 139) is a testament to this. All of the recipes in the book call for extra-virgin olive oil, which you may use to shallow-fry meats, vegetables, and cheeses. However, you may also use regular olive oil or avocado oil for high heat, if you prefer.

Tips for Cooking and Eating with Gusto

Get in the Mood

Play some of your favorite music. Light some candles. Smell the food. Taste the food. Appreciate the food. Use all of your senses. The joy of cooking comes from being in the present. Use the freshest and most aromatic ingredients you can find. Few things are as pleasurable as filling your kitchen with the smell of fresh seasonal citrus on a dull winter's day.

Get Acquainted

Read the entire recipe before beginning to make it. This will give you knowledge of what comes next. It will also make the cooking process quicker and more relaxing.

Easy Cleanup

Keep your surfaces clean and clear so that you can better focus on the food. For instance, when handling pomegranates, seed them in a large bowl filled with water inside your sink. Then strain everything through a strainer to catch the arils. This will prevent your kitchen from looking like a crime scene. Removing any extra dishes or utensils from your work area will prevent you from feeling overwhelmed. Overall, less clutter equates to less chaos when cooking.

Use Your Instincts

If you like or dislike a certain spice, add a bit extra or skip it altogether. If you prefer certain herbs, use the ones you like. Substitute parsley for cilantro, for example. Look over the main ingredients before you make a recipe and alter the herbs, aromatics, and spices to your taste.

Salt

Get accustomed to feeling the salt and getting comfortable with the amounts you hold. Salt is personal, so even though I have provided the amounts that I use in my kitchen, do adjust them to your liking. If you have slightly oversalted a dish and it is still repairable, add more liquid. You can also downplay the salt by adding more lemon juice, vinegar, sugar, or chili as is relevant to the flavors in the recipe.

Hospitality

This is one of the most important components of the Mediterranean style of eating. The happiest and healthiest societies in the world share the values of being around others and feeling a strong sense of community. Bring your favorite people to gather around your table. Also, invite new guests. The best way to embrace another culture, besides travel, is through food. Good food reminds us of the fact that we have more that unites us than divides us. So, live, laugh, and relish the moment.

Making Ahead

Get in the habit of preparing all of the ingredients needed in the recipe ahead of time. Lay them out in your kitchen in the order of the ingredients list. When entertaining, prepare as many components of the meal as possible beforehand. You want to enjoy your company, not be hidden away in the kitchen. Keep batches of frozen foods such as sofrito ready for instant injections of gusto into your food. Cookie doughs such as the one for Alfajores with Cajeta (page 144) can be kept frozen, making them perfect for entertaining last-minute guests. Most doughs can also be made in advance.

Mindfulness

Eat slowly and savor the moment. Taste the food and be mindful of the present. This is better for you and those around you. In Spain, there is a word for the time spent at the table after a meal—*sobremesa*. In this period, time stops, and attention is placed on contemplating the day, embracing your guests, and digesting the food.

Mezze

Mezze stems from the Arabic word *mezze*, meaning "to relish small bites." The mezze tradition is the very definition of hospitality. Similar to tapas and antipasti, small mezze dishes are presented before a meal in a most intimate matter, fueling appetites and sparking conversations. Mezze is more than a type of plate; it represents a lifestyle centered on conviviality. The tapas culture, which was born in Andalusia, shares many of the attributes of the mezze culture of the eastern Mediterranean. And many Spanish starters are similar to the mezze dishes served in the Levant. Fried eggplants with honey or molasses (page 32) and other vegetable fritters, olives, cheeses, dips, and tapenade are all examples of the shared flavors throughout the Mediterranean. This style of eating is indeed a feast for the eyes and joy for the soul. The excitement that comes from knowing that the next bite will be completely different from the last is what mezze culture is about. Plenty of small, delectable plates made for sharing and creating conversation are always welcomed.

The mezze dishes in this chapter are some of the most essential ones in my kitchen. Some are perfect for entertaining, and others are versatile additions to everyday meals. The Muhammara—Roasted Red Pepper Dip (page 23) is vibrant, sweet, and earthy. Its flavor profile completes a table of savory starters. The Hummus Beiruti—Fava Bean and Herb Hummus (page 19) is a fresh take on hummus that is delicious eaten alone or spread inside of a sandwich. A batch of fierce potatoes (page 31) may be served as a starter or side to your main meal. The Sesame-Encrusted Halloumi with Honey Sauce (page 36) is salty, sweet, tangy, and anything but boring. What all of these dishes have in common is that they are beautiful and enticing, making them perfect for the beginning of a feast.

Growing up, a table full of mezze would conjure many memories and feelings of nostalgia. They would center on the hummus that I would have in Jaffa during my childhood summers, the breads reminiscent of those freshly baked in Palestinian taboon ovens, the fried eggplant of bustling southern Spanish restaurants, and the small dishes served with seafood along the Mediterranean coast.

The mezze course is meant to unite and relax people. You can enjoy an evening eating mezze dishes with a stranger and already feel like you know them a bit more afterward. Mezze is where conversations begin and where formality ends. When we share plates with each other, in the very intimate manner of this act, we are essentially letting our guards down. We are one.

Cannellini Bean Dip with Mushrooms

Serves 4

Creamy, garlicky cannellini beans topped with sautéed mushrooms and herbs make this starter absolutely addictive. The rustic nature of this dish reminds me of the Canaanite landscape that I was so used to seeing while living in the Levant. Indeed, that was where I first combined mushrooms with white beans and joyfully relished the moment. This is an excellent dip to serve alongside other starters before a feast. But it is equally pleasing on its own with some pita crisps and a salad to round it out.

For the Puree

3 tbsp (45 ml) fresh lemon juice

3 large cloves garlic, finely minced

½ tsp fine sea salt, plus more to taste

2 cups (260 g) cannellini beans, canned or cooked

⅓ cup (60 g) crumbled feta (thick and buttery variety)

½ cup (80 g) thick full-fat Turkish or Greek yogurt

1 tbsp (15 ml) extra-virgin olive oil

For the Mushroom Mixture

6 tbsp (90 ml) extra-virgin olive oil, divided

6 shallots or 1 medium onion, thinly sliced

½ tsp fine sea salt plus a pinch, divided

12 baby bella or cremini mushrooms, halved

2 large cloves garlic, finely minced

Pinch of ground nutmeg

2 thyme sprigs

Freshly ground black pepper

For Garnish

Aleppo chili flakes or other dried chili variety

Handful of parsley, coarsely chopped

Thyme

Olive oil

Dukkah

Warm, crisp bread, for serving

For the puree, combine the lemon juice, minced garlic, and salt in a small bowl, stir together, and leave to sit for 10 minutes. Meanwhile, place the beans in a strainer and rinse them well. Be sure to remove as much liquid as possible. Place the beans in your food processor and add the feta, lemon juice and garlic mixture, yogurt, and olive oil. Pulse the ingredients until smooth, add salt to taste, and set aside.

To make the mushroom mixture, add 3 tablespoons (45 ml) of olive oil to a large pan over medium heat and bring to a sizzle. Stir in the sliced shallots and ½ teaspoon of salt. Bring the heat down to low and sauté while stirring often for about 10 minutes, or until the shallots are soft and golden brown in color. Remove the shallots from the heat and set aside. Add another 3 tablespoons (45 ml) of olive oil to the pan and add the mushrooms, garlic, nutmeg, thyme, and black pepper. Set the heat to medium-high and sauté until cooked, 5 to 7 minutes, stirring often. Add a generous pinch of salt after the mushrooms are cooked. This will allow the mushrooms to brown and not release too much liquid during cooking.

Spoon the cannellini mixture onto a serving plate or shallow bowl and top with the mushroom mixture. Sprinkle chili flakes, parsley, thyme, olive oil, and dukkah over the top. Serve with warm, crisp bread.

Variation: *Fava beans also pair well with mushrooms. I like to use frozen, peeled fava beans in this dish. Before using the fava beans in the recipe, cook them for about 10 minutes in a medium pan over medium-high heat with a generous pinch of salt and 2 to 3 tablespoons (30 to 45 ml) of olive oil. Then substitute the same amount of fava for the cannellini and proceed with the recipe.*

Spice Routes: Dukkah is an ancient Egyptian spice mix with citrusy and nutty notes. It pairs well with the earthy and deep flavors of legumes and mushrooms.

Hummus Beiruti– Fava Bean and Herb Hummus

Serves 4

1 tsp fine sea salt

¼ cup (60 ml) lemon juice

3 large cloves garlic, finely minced

1 cup (110 g) frozen green fava beans, peeled and thawed

2 cups (340 g) garbanzo beans, cooked or canned, drained (see Notes)

⅔ cup (140 g) tahini

½ tsp ground cumin

2 tbsp (30 ml) extra-virgin olive oil, plus more for topping

2–4 tbsp (30–60 ml) cold water

Handful of fresh parsley, finely chopped, plus more for topping

Small handful of fresh mint, finely chopped, plus more for topping

1 tsp Aleppo chili flakes, plus more for topping

Paprika, for topping

Pine nuts, toasted, for topping

There will never be too many recipes for hummus. There are endless ways to enjoy this delicious dip that I trace back to home—creamy, chunky, fresh, savory, light, infused, classic, and the list goes on. This recipe, in particular, is one that hummus lovers should have in their recipe arsenal. Known as hummus Beiruti, it was named after Lebanese migrants who introduced this dish to Latin America in the early 1900s. I love the textures and contrasts between the fresh fava and creamy garbanzo beans. Fresh herbs are blended with the hummus to add life, vibrance, and flavor. For convenience, I have a preference for good-quality canned garbanzo beans in this recipe, making this dip quickly accessible during the most demanding times.

Combine the salt, lemon juice, and garlic in a small bowl, and set aside for 15 minutes. This will reduce the pungency of the garlic. In the meantime, place the fava beans in a small pot, cover with water, bring to a simmer, and cook for about 10 minutes, or until tender. Do the same with the garbanzo beans if canned. Drain and set aside.

In a high-powered blender, add the garbanzos, reserving a few for topping, to the lemon-garlic mixture and blend well. Add the tahini, cumin, and olive oil and blend just until well combined to keep the hummus slightly chunky. Add just enough of the cold water to achieve the consistency that you prefer. Add the fresh parsley, mint, chili flakes, and 1 cup (170 g) of the cooked fava beans, reserving a few for topping. Pulse until well combined but chunky. Spoon the hummus into a large serving bowl, and top with olive oil, the remaining fava beans, the remaining garbanzos, parsley, mint, chili flakes, a sprinkle of paprika, and toasted pine nuts.

Notes: *If you are using dried garbanzo beans, place them in a medium bowl and cover the legumes with about 3 inches (8 cm) of water. Stir in a teaspoon of baking soda and leave to soak overnight. Drain and rinse the next day. Then place the soaked garbanzo beans in a medium pot of boiling water over medium-high heat, with enough water to cover the beans by 4 inches (10 cm). Add ½ teaspoon of baking soda and ½ teaspoon of fine sea salt and cook for about 1½ hours, or until the garbanzos are very soft and even overcooked. Drain them well and set aside until you use them.*

Even though I prefer to cook my garbanzos, canned or jarred garbanzos are perfectly adequate substitutes and ones that I often use when I am pressed for time.

Tip: *If you need to thin out the hummus to get a creamier consistency, stream cold water into the blender or food processor until you get the texture you want.*

Roasted Carrot and Chili Hummus

Serves 4

This colorful hummus is inspired by the warm, sweet, and spicy flavors of North African cuisine. Turn up the heat by keeping the rinds and seeds of the chili and adding more shatta or harissa, if you like. The crispy garbanzos add a lovely crunch to the final dish. Adjust the toppings to your liking and serve with warm pita bread.

For the Hummus

4 tbsp (60 ml) extra-virgin olive oil, divided

2 large carrots, sliced into ¼-inch (6-mm)-thick pieces

6 large cloves garlic, whole

1 medium red chili (mild variety), halved and seeded

½ cup (120 g) tahini

⅔ cup (160 ml) fresh lemon juice

2 cups (340 g) garbanzo beans, cooked or canned, well drained

⅛ tsp turmeric

½ tsp ground cumin

1 tsp fine sea salt, or to taste

2–5 tbsp (30–75 ml) water

For the Crispy Garbanzo Topping

1 tbsp (15 ml) extra-virgin olive oil

½ cup (85 g) garbanzo beans, cooked or canned, drained

½ tsp ground cumin

¼ tsp pimentón dulce

¼ tsp chili flakes

1 tsp sweet chili sauce

⅛ tsp fine sea salt

⅛ tsp ground turmeric

For Garnish

Olive oil

Pinch of chili flakes, optional

Sweet chili sauce, shatta, or harissa

Dukkah

Fresh parsley

Pine nuts, toasted

Preheat the oven to 400°F (200°C). Add 1 tablespoon (15 ml) of olive oil, the sliced carrots, garlic, and red chili to a small roasting pan and toss them together. Roast the vegetables for about 25 minutes, or until the carrot pieces are lightly golden and tender. Toss the vegetables halfway through for even roasting. Leave to cool.

In a food processor or very high-powered blender, pulse together the tahini and lemon juice until smooth. Add the cooked vegetables, garbanzo beans, turmeric, cumin, salt, 3 tablespoons (45 ml) of olive oil, and 2 tablespoons (30 ml) of water. Blend again until smooth. Check your consistency and if necessary, add 1 to 3 tablespoons (15 to 45 ml) of cold water until you get your desired texture. The amount of liquid you need will differ depending on how much water your garbanzos have retained. Check for salt and seasoning and adjust to your liking.

To make the crispy garbanzo bean topping, heat a large pan over medium-high heat, add the olive oil, and bring to a sizzle. Add the garbanzos and toss with the cumin, pimentón, chili flakes, chili sauce, salt, and turmeric. Cook over medium-high heat until crispy, 5 to 8 minutes.

Spoon the hummus into a serving dish and top with olive oil, chili flakes if desired, chili sauce, dukkah, fresh parsley, crispy garbanzos, and toasted pine nuts. This hummus keeps well chilled in an airtight container for 2 to 3 days.

Spice Routes: With the addition of dukkah, the flavors of sweet carrots, citrusy coriander, and savory cumin come together in natural harmony. Aleppo chili rounds out these flavors with heat and depth.

Muhammara–Roasted Red Pepper Dip

Serves 4

3 large red bell peppers, seeds removed, cut into 1" (2.5-cm) strips

¼ cup (60 ml) extra-virgin olive oil, divided, plus more for topping

Pinch plus ½ tsp fine sea salt, divided

2 shallots or ½ medium onion, finely chopped

½ tsp ground cumin

½ tsp ground 7 spice

Freshly ground black pepper, to taste

½ tsp Aleppo chili flakes or regular chili flakes

2 tsp (10 g) sweet chili sauce or shatta

2 tbsp (42 g) pomegranate molasses

1 tbsp (16 g) tomato paste

1 tbsp (15 ml) fresh lemon juice

7 sun-dried tomatoes, coarsely chopped

1½ cups (170 g) walnuts, toasted (see Tip)

For Garnish

Pomegranate molasses

Chili flakes

Pomegranate seeds

Black and white sesame seeds

Chopped parsley

This rich dip hails from Aleppo, Syria, and is quite popular in south-central Turkey. Red pepper is roasted or grilled until soft and charred, peeled, and then blended with spices, pomegranate, chili, and walnuts. Traditionally, fine bulgur is added to the dip, but I prefer not to downplay the intensity of the roasted red pepper.

Preheat the oven to 425°F (220°C). Toss the red pepper with 1 tablespoon (15 ml) of olive oil and a pinch of salt. Arrange the strips skin side up on a roasting tray. Roast for 25 to 30 minutes, or until the peppers are blistered and slightly charred, flipping them halfway through. Cool them for at least 10 minutes before blending in the food processor.

In the food processor, add the roasted red pepper, shallots, cumin, 7 spice, ½ teaspoon salt, pepper, chili flakes, chili sauce, pomegranate molasses, tomato paste, lemon juice, 3 tablespoons (45 ml) of olive oil, sun-dried tomatoes, and walnuts, reserving three walnuts for topping. Pulse the ingredients until smooth. Spoon the dip into a bowl and top with walnuts and a generous drizzle of olive oil. Additional topping options include pomegranate molasses, chili flakes, pomegranate seeds, black and white sesame seeds, and chopped parsley. Enjoy right away or chill in the refrigerator until serving. Serve alongside other mezze dishes and bread for dipping.

Tip: *Toast the walnuts in a 350°F (180°C) oven for 10 minutes, tossing halfway through. Allow them to cool for 5 minutes before using them in the recipe.*

Spice Routes: Aleppo chili is a great complement to the sweetness of the peppers. Its smokiness adds both depth and balance to this dish. It has just the perfect amount of heat, allowing you to use a generous quantity without the added spiciness that comes with other chili varieties.

Charred Zucchini, Yogurt, and Mint Dip

Serves 4

2 large cloves garlic, finely minced

2 tbsp (30 ml) lemon juice

½ tsp fine sea salt plus a pinch, divided

4–5 medium zucchini, halved vertically

2 tbsp (30 ml) extra-virgin olive oil, divided, plus more for topping

½ cup (60 g) pine nuts or walnuts, toasted and finely crushed

Handful of fresh mint, finely chopped

½ cup (115 g) plain yogurt, drained at room temperature for 1–2 hours (see Tip), or Turkish yogurt

¼ cup (36 g) crumbled creamy feta cheese

For Garnish

Shaved zucchini

Toasted pine nuts

Dried mint

Aleppo chili flakes

The combination of yogurt and mint is used in an abundance of ways in Mediterranean cooking. In this dip, I add roasted zucchini and nuts for a fresh and flavorful dip. I like to use Turkish yogurt when I can find it as it is already moderately thick, but not so much as Greek yogurt. Most of the time, however, I simply place plain yogurt on a fine mesh strainer lined with a layer of cheesecloth and leave it out at room temperature for an hour or two before using.

Combine the garlic, lemon juice, and ½ teaspoon of salt in a small bowl and set aside for at least 10 minutes before using.

Preheat the oven to 425°F (220°C) and place the zucchini on a roasting tray. Brush with 1 tablespoon (15 ml) of olive oil and season with a pinch of salt. Roast the zucchini for 25 to 30 minutes, skin side up, until lightly golden. Alternatively, place the zucchini under a low broiler until charred and lightly browned, about 15 minutes, flipping halfway through.

Mash the roasted zucchini in a colander to remove excess liquid and then spoon it into a bowl. Remove any brown bits from the zucchini and add the nuts, mint, yogurt, feta, 1 tablespoon (15 ml) of olive oil, and the garlic, lemon juice, and salt mixture. Mix the ingredients with a fork to combine. You may also pulse the ingredients in a food processor until well blended. Blend to the consistency of your liking. Spoon the dip into a serving bowl and top with olive oil, shaved zucchini slices, toasted pine nuts, mint, and chili.

Tip: To strain the yogurt, line a sieve with a fine mesh cloth and place over a bowl to catch any liquid. Spoon the yogurt inside and strain for 1 to 2 hours.

Roasted Sweet Potato and Lentil Soup with Maple-Tahini Sauce

Serves 4

This has been my go-to soup for many years now. It is creamy and satisfying and simply feels good to eat. Sweet potato, pumpkin, and squash are all wonderful with tahini. I will always relish this combination, especially in autumn, when orange vegetables are bursting with flavor.

3 sweet potatoes, cut into cubes

4 tbsp (60 ml) extra-virgin olive oil, divided

2¼ tsp (11 g) fine sea salt, divided, plus more for the onions

Freshly ground black pepper

1 large onion, finely chopped

1 large carrot, finely diced

1 medium tart apple such as Granny Smith, peeled and diced

1 tsp pimentón dulce or sweet paprika

½ tsp ground turmeric

1 tsp ground cumin

Pinch of ground nutmeg

2 large cloves garlic, finely minced

5 cups (1.2 L) good vegetable or chicken stock

1 cup (150 g) red lentils, soaked and well rinsed

Pumpkin and sunflower seeds, toasted, for topping

Za'atar, for topping

For the Sauce

¼ cup (60 g) tahini

¼ cup (60 ml) lemon juice

1 tbsp (21 g) maple syrup

Pinch of cinnamon

Pinch of fine sea salt

Preheat the oven to 425°F (220°C) and place the sweet potatoes onto a large baking tray. Toss the potatoes with 1 tablespoon (15 ml) of olive oil, ½ teaspoon of salt, and a good grinding of black pepper. Bake them for 25 to 30 minutes, or until tender and golden around the edges. In the meantime, heat a skillet over medium-low heat, sauté the onion with 3 tablespoons (45 ml) of olive oil and a generous sprinkle of salt until soft and transparent, about 10 minutes. Stir in the carrot, apple, pimentón, turmeric, cumin, nutmeg, garlic, and another grinding of black pepper. Cook for another 5 minutes. Then, add the stock and bring it to a simmer. Add the lentils and 1¾ teaspoons (9 g) of salt, reduce the heat to low, cover, and cook for 20 minutes. Stir the roasted potatoes into the soup and blend using an immersion blender or in batches with a stand blender. Check the soup for seasoning and set aside.

For the sauce, combine the tahini and lemon juice in a small bowl and mix until smooth. Stir in the maple syrup, cinnamon, and sea salt and mix until well combined. To serve the soup, top with the maple-tahini sauce, pumpkin seeds, sunflower seeds, and za'atar.

Green Rutabaga and Spinach Soup

Serves 4–6

Fall is the season for soups, and coincidentally, rutabaga is also harvested during this time of year. Its flavor is mild, buttery, and sweet. When paired with fresh greens, it makes for an earthy, warm, and satisfying bowl of yum. The soup is wholesome, but it is also fresh and cleansing. A pot of this on a chilly winter's day will feel like the most comforting hug.

Begin by caramelizing the leeks. Heat the olive oil in a medium pot over medium heat and bring it to a sizzle. Add the leeks and season with a generous pinch of salt. Stir the leeks often and sauté until soft and lightly golden, 10 to 12 minutes.

Add the rutabaga and cook for another 5 minutes while stirring. Then add the green lentils, 1¼ teaspoons (7 g) of salt, pepper, cayenne, and cumin then stir. Add the vegetable broth and bay leaf, bring to a simmer, reduce the heat to low, cover and cook for 20 minutes, or until the lentils are tender.

Remove and discard the bay leaf and stir in the spinach. Blend using an immersion blender or carefully in batches using a stand blender. Stir in the parsley and lemon juice. Serve topped with dukkah, olive oil, parsley, and chili flakes.

For the Soup

3 tbsp (45 ml) extra-virgin olive oil

2 leeks, white and light green parts, finely chopped

Pinch plus 1¼ tsp (7 g) fine sea salt, divided

½ large rutabaga, diced

1 cup (180 g) green lentils, rinsed, soaked for 30 minutes and drained

Freshly ground black pepper

⅛ tsp cayenne pepper

½ tsp ground cumin

6 cups (1.4 L) vegetable broth

1 bay leaf

3 cups (140 g) packed baby spinach, purslane, or a combination of both

½ cup (10 g) parsley

¼ cup (60 ml) lemon juice

For Garnish

Dukkah

Olive oil

Parsley

Aleppo chili flakes

Fierce Baby Potatoes with Spices, Chili, and Herbs

Serves 4

In Spanish and Latin cuisines, they call the combination of crispy potatoes, chili, and garlic patatas bravas, or "fierce potatoes." In Arabic, a starter with similar ingredients but a slightly different technique is called batata harra, meaning "spicy potatoes." Both versions are traditionally fried, but they are equally delicious roasted. In the Canary Islands, where my grandfather, Antonio, was originally from, potatoes are served in many flavorful ways. A specialty there is wrinkled potatoes with red and green sauces. Here is my twist on the recipe. It calls for a green sauce known as mojo verde. Keep the seeds and membranes of the chili in the sauce if you can handle the heat.

For the Potatoes

20 baby or creamer potatoes, cut into halves

2 tbsp (30 ml) extra-virgin olive oil

1 tsp fine sea salt

Freshly ground pepper

¼ tsp cayenne pepper

1 tsp cumin seeds, coarsely crushed

2 tsp (6 g) coriander seeds, coarsely crushed

4 sprigs fresh thyme

¼ tsp pimentón dulce, for topping

For the Green Sauce or Mojo Verde

3 tbsp (45 ml) lemon juice

2 tsp (10 ml) apple cider vinegar

1 cup (20 g) cilantro

½ cup (10 g) parsley

3 cloves garlic, finely minced

1 medium green jalapeño chili, seeds and membrane removed, minced

⅛ tsp fine sea salt

⅛ tsp ground cumin

¼ cup (60 ml) extra-virgin olive oil

Preheat your oven to 425°F (220°C) and spread the potatoes onto a large baking sheet. Top them with the olive oil, salt, pepper, cayenne, cumin, coriander, thyme, and pimentón dulce. Toss the potatoes with the seasonings and arrange them cut side down on the baking sheet. Roast them for 20 to 25 minutes, or until golden.

Meanwhile, prepare your green sauce. Add the lemon juice, vinegar, cilantro, parsley, garlic, chili, salt, cumin, and olive oil to a food processor or blender and pulse until smooth. Set the sauce aside until serving the potatoes. When the potatoes are ready, brush them with the green sauce and enjoy at once.

Fried Eggplant with Carob-Maple Sauce

Serves 4

Fried eggplants with honey are a popular tapa in southern Spain. In Andalusia, Seville, and Malaga, in particular, the dish is a relic of a Moorish past. Molasses or miel de caña is what was traditionally used. Most versions, however, will use honey. In this twist, I like to combine carob and maple or honey for a deep, smoky, and sweet-flavored sauce. I also prefer frying the strips for this recipe, which results in melt-in-your-mouth bites. Soaking the eggplant in water before cooking prevents it from absorbing too much oil. Top with parsley, Urfa chili, crushed almonds, and sesame.

2 tsp (10 g) fine sea salt, plus a pinch, divided

2 medium eggplants, cut into 3½ x 1" (9 x 2.5–cm) strips or sliced into rounds

⅔ cup (84 g) all-purpose flour

Canola or sunflower oil, for frying

3 tbsp (45 ml) carob syrup

1 tbsp (21 g) maple syrup or honey

2 tsp (10 ml) lemon juice

Pinch of Urfa chili

For Garnish

Sea salt flakes

Generous pinch of Urfa chili

Handful of parsley, finely chopped

Blanched almonds, toasted and crushed

Toasted sesame seeds

Lemon wedges

Fill a large bowl with cold water and stir in the salt. Let the eggplant sit in the water for 40 minutes. This will help reduce both acidity and oil absorption. Drain the eggplant strips, pat them dry with a paper towel, season with a generous sprinkle of salt, and coat in the flour.

Place a large pot or pan over medium-high heat and fill it with about 2 inches (5 cm) of oil. Once the oil reaches 375°F (190°C), or it starts to sizzle when you drop some flour inside, carefully arrange the eggplant pieces in the pot. Fry for about 3 minutes on each side, or until crisp and golden brown. Place on a paper towel to dry.

Add the carob syrup, maple syrup, lemon juice, Urfa chili, and a pinch of salt to a small bowl and mix together to combine. To serve, drizzle the sauce over the eggplant fritters and sprinkle with sea salt flakes, Urfa chili, parsley, crushed almond, and sesame seeds, with lemon wedges for garnish. Alternatively, serve the carob-maple sauce on the side as dip.

Spice Routes: Urfa chili, which gets its name from the Turkish city it comes from, works really well with carob. Its flavor can be described as mild, smoky, and deep. Carob, which hails from the Mediterranean parts of the Middle East, is sweet, deep, and chocolate-like in flavor. Both flavors are intense but come together wonderfully for a sweet and spicy profile.

Olive, Eggplant, Pepper, and Sun-Dried Tomato Caponata

Serves 4

¼ cup (60 ml) extra-virgin olive oil, divided

1 medium eggplant, peeled and cubed

½ tsp fine sea salt, plus more to taste

1 large sweet onion such as Vidalia, finely chopped

1 large red bell pepper, seeds removed, chopped

3 large cloves garlic, finely minced

6 Manzanilla or cured black olives, seeds removed, chopped

1 anchovy fillet, finely minced

2 tbsp (32 g) tomato paste

2 tsp (10 ml) balsamic vinegar

2 tsp (11 g) pomegranate molasses

1 tbsp (15 ml) lemon juice

½ cup (10 g) parsley, finely chopped, plus more for topping

Toasted pine nuts, for topping

There are versions of caponata or eggplant dip throughout the Mediterranean, all with different names. From Southern Italy, Sicily in particular, to Tunisia to Lebanon and Palestine, this small dish is highly regarded as a starter. Cooking methods and ingredients vary by region, but the concept is all too similar. Pan-sizzle the eggplant until it is juicy and caramelized, mash it, and then combine it with bits of flavor. This is one of those dishes that takes me places. On this occasion, it brings me near Sicily's wondrous coast where people gather and enjoy small bites. The key to good caponata-style dishes like these is to cook the eggplant separately. Give this glorious vegetable the love it deserves.

Add 3 tablespoons (45 ml) of olive oil to a large pan over medium-high heat. Once the oil is hot enough so that a piece of eggplant starts to sizzle, add the rest of the eggplant and toss to coat it in the oil. Season with the salt and cook while stirring often for 12 to 15 minutes, or until golden. Set aside.

Add another tablespoon (15 ml) of olive oil to the pan and stir in the onion, red pepper, and a pinch of salt. Reduce the heat to medium-low and cook the vegetables until they are soft, for 10 to 12 minutes, stirring often. Stir in the garlic, olives, anchovy, tomato paste, and a generous pinch of salt and sauté for an additional 15 minutes over medium heat. Stir in the balsamic vinegar, pomegranate molasses, lemon juice, and parsley. Adjust the seasoning to taste and spoon the caponata into a serving bowl. Top with pine nuts and fresh parsley. Enjoy at once or refrigerate overnight and enjoy the next day.

Sesame-Encrusted Halloumi with Honey Sauce

Serves 4

Halloumi is a satisfyingly chewy and delicious Mediterranean cheese traditionally enjoyed throughout Cyprus, Greece, Turkey, and the Levant. It has a salty and deep flavor that is the result of the mixture of sheep and goat milk. Halloumi's high melting point makes it the perfect cheese to fry or panfry. One of my favorite ways to serve it is coated with sesame seeds and orange zest and drizzled with honey.

3 tbsp (60 g) orange blossom honey

3 tbsp (45 ml) orange juice

1 egg white, beaten

2 tsp (2 g) freshly grated orange zest

2 tbsp (18 g) white sesame seeds

1 tbsp (9 g) black sesame seeds

½ lb (230 g) halloumi, cut into squares

1 tbsp (15 ml) extra-virgin olive oil

For Garnish

¼ tsp Aleppo chili flakes

Lemon or orange wedges

Mint leaves

Combine the honey and orange juice in a medium saucepan and place it over medium-high heat. Stir together and simmer for about 3 minutes, or until the sauce thickens and resembles a light syrup. Remove from the heat and set aside.

Add the egg white and orange zest to a medium bowl and mix to combine. Place the white and black sesame seeds in a separate bowl. Brush the halloumi with the egg white and then press a piece of halloumi into the seeds to cover it. Flip to coat the other side and repeat with the rest of the halloumi. Place a skillet over medium-low heat, add the olive oil to coat the pan, and place the halloumi in the pan. Panfry the cheese for about 2 minutes on each side, or until golden. Drizzle the cheese with the honey sauce and top with chili flakes, fresh lemon, and mint. Enjoy right away.

Baked Portobello Mushrooms Stuffed with Freekeh

Serves 4

It has always seemed to me that mushrooms and freekeh were made for one another. The smoky flavor of the grain works so well with the savory and umami taste of mushrooms. I first enjoyed a freekeh-style risotto dish in an elegant restaurant called Harir, overlooking the Palestinian olive groves. The restaurant no longer stands, but it inspired me to play with traditional flavors. This is one of the few instances where I use the combination of cream, butter, and parmesan, but they are musts in this recipe, making for creamy, savory, risotto-style freekeh. If you need this dish to be dairy-free, skip the cream and use more olive oil in place of the butter. Or use dairy-free butter, cream, and cheese substitutes. I particularly love this flavor profile with my pomegranate and sumac chicken recipe (page 61).

7 tbsp (105 ml) extra-virgin olive oil, divided

1 medium onion, finely chopped

1 medium rib celery, finely chopped

Pinch plus ¾ tsp fine sea salt, divided

4 large cloves garlic, finely minced, divided

1 cup (160 g) freekeh, rinsed

2½ cups (600 ml) hot good vegetable or chicken stock

1 tbsp (14 g) salted butter

½ cup (45 g) grated parmesan cheese, plus more for topping

Pinch of nutmeg

Handful of parsley, finely chopped, plus more for topping

20 medium portobello stuffing mushrooms, stems removed

Chives, finely chopped, for topping

Place a medium pot over medium heat and add 3 tablespoons (45 ml) of olive oil. When the oil is hot, stir in the onion, celery, and a pinch of salt. Sauté the vegetables for about 10 minutes, or until the onion is soft and transparent. Add 2 cloves of garlic and cook for another 2 minutes, while stirring. Stir in the freekeh and cook it for another 3 minutes. Add the hot stock and ¾ teaspoon of salt and bring the pot to a simmer, reduce the heat to low, and cook the freekeh for 22 to 25 minutes, or until tender to the bite. Stir in the butter, parmesan, nutmeg, and parsley. Set aside.

Preheat the oven to 400°F (200°C) and place the mushrooms in a large bowl. Add 4 tablespoons (60 ml) of olive oil and 2 cloves of minced garlic. Toss the mushrooms to coat them in the fragrant oil and arrange them top down onto a large baking tray. Stuff each mushroom with a generous amount of the freekeh filling, about a generous tablespoon (15 g). Bake the stuffed mushrooms for 16 to 18 minutes. Top with grated parmesan, parsley, and fresh chives.

Meat and Poultry

Meat and poultry play an important role in the culinary landscape of the Mediterranean. Lamb, veal, beef, chicken, and game birds such as pigeon and quail have been the meats of choice. But historically, meat was reserved for special occasions. In the Levant, for example, many families would serve meat once a week because it was not affordable to indulge in it more often. Vegetables, ancient grains, and legume-based dishes were the norm. Today, modern trends are leaning toward this ideal. And it makes sense. Eat less meat of better quality and reserve it for occasions. This is not only more sustainable, but better for our well-being.

When the time comes to enjoy good-quality meat, make the most of it. Treat the meat with respect and cook it with joy. I find that this is best carried out through slow-cooked stews, which require very little effort for maximum reward. Very little can go wrong when you leave a pot of meat such as the Braised Lamb Shanks with Tamarind (page 53) slowly simmering away or roasting. And cooked long enough, the result is fall-off-the-bone, tender, juicy goodness.

Traybakes such as the Roasted Chicken Thighs with Preserved Lemon, Dates, and Honey (page 58) and Roasted Chicken with Pomegranate Glaze and Sumac (page 61) are delicious express options given that the meat is marinated for a couple of hours, or better yet, overnight. Simply place the contents of the recipe in a ziplock bag, seal tightly, and let the ingredients work their magic. The next day, transfer the meat and any released juices to a baking tray and pop it in the oven for about an hour before dinner.

A Note on "Fusion" and Flavor

The term *fusion cuisine* carries a negative connotation—seen often as describing a lazy way of recipe development that doesn't respect culture, tradition, or flavor harmony. But it is important to acknowledge that recipes have developed this way throughout the millennia. I am not fond of the term *fusion cuisine* because it is often associated with fusing two very different groups of flavors that do not marry well. For example, I do not recommend combining hummus with southeast Asian flavors such as lemongrass and ginger. However, add some sazón and sofrito to kibbeh, or *kippeh* as it is known in the Latin world, and you have got some serious flavor going. The idea is to combine flavors that harmoniously flow with one another and that complement each other. It is important to understand the cultural context of ingredients to pair them in harmonious ways.

This is how food and recipes evolved throughout the past centuries. A case in point are the cuisines of Andalusia. When the Moors occupied the south of Spain from 792 to 1400, a period also known as the Golden Age, they brought with them their aromatic spices, almonds, pomegranates, eggplants, sugar preservation techniques, rice-frying techniques, pickling techniques, agricultural techniques, and the list goes on. Their marks on Spain's gastronomy along with those of Sicily, Malta, and Portugal are still seen today. The use of almonds, raisins, saffron, eggplant, and orange in cooking is just an example of the fusions that happened with time. Techniques such as escabeche and molding meat to make meatballs are also remnants of a Moorish past.

Flavor migrations in Latin America have taken place even recently. Consider Mexican tacos Árabes, lamb tacos (page 44), the result of Lebanese migration to Puebla and Jalisco, Mexico, in the 1800s. A Mexican version of the original lamb shawarma was created with chipotle sauce and a taco wrap. Another example is *jocoque*, the Mexican term for Levantine-style strained yogurt, or labneh, popular in Mexico far longer than in the United States.

In America and Britain, notable fusions happened with Mexican, Chinese, Italian, and Indian cooking—they became Westernized. Chimichangas, orange chicken, chicken parmesan, and chicken tikka masala are some examples. So that brings us to the question of authenticity. How authentic are dishes when they have been the subject of various influences? Food evolves with time. Recipes evolve. Palates adapt. I love this rich intermingling of cultures. I have experienced it on a personal level and seen how well it works.

A Note on Sweet and Sour and Fruit Marinades

Marinades and sauces made from fruit juices have been used for cooking meats since ancient times. The combination of sweet and sour was especially prevalent in the Levantine part of the Mediterranean during the Middle Ages. Lamb stews with quince or orange juice were common. There are many recipes in *The Anonymous Andalusian Cookbook*, written in Valencia during the 13th century, that focus on this way of cooking.

In the Levant, pomegranate molasses and tamarind paste, in particular, have always been popular ingredients for meat dishes. From Syria to Turkey, especially around the Gaziantep and Aleppo border, sweet and savory combinations are celebrated.

Vinegar was an essential ingredient in meat dishes of Andalusian cuisine. It went hand in hand with the sweet element provided by fruits. The lovely acidity of vinegar in a hearty stew creates gusto and complexity and adds that tang needed for the perfect balance of flavors.

Today, cooking with fruit juices feels natural to me. It tastes like home. It adds freshness, depth, and life. The vibrant color of pomegranate in roasted chicken is enough to wake the senses. It is especially pleasurable in the fall. As the colors outdoors begin to fade away, the vibrancy of fall produce arrives to enliven our days.

Fruits that complement meat dishes include pomegranate, orange, apricot, cherries, loquat, quince, dates, apples, pears, and tamarind.

Tacos Árabes– Lamb Tacos with Chipotle Sauce

Serves 4

These Mexican/Middle Eastern tacos hail from Puebla, Mexico. Lebanese, Syrian, and Palestinian migrants brought the concept of shawarma to Mexico around the 1800s and fused it with local flavors. So you had the Levantine style of cooking meat on a vertical roaster, Mexican sauces such as chipotle, and breads such as pita or tortillas. Given that tacos and shawarma were all too similar, the name tacos Árabes was inevitable. These tacos are perfect for a gathering or cooking for friends and family. If you can find boneless lamb shoulder and have your butcher thinly slice it, you may use it with the marinade and then grill it. Essentially, you may use your favorite cut of lamb and cook it as you like. Just separate the meat from the bone and chop it before serving. I have used lamb ribs in this recipe. You may slow cook them or grill them to your preferred level of doneness.

For the Lamb Tacos

½ cup (120 ml) orange juice

4 tbsp (60 ml) lime juice

2 tbsp (30 ml) apple cider vinegar

¼ cup (60 ml) extra-virgin olive oil

1 tsp pimentón dulce or smoked paprika

1 tsp 7 spice

1 tsp ground cumin

1 tsp ground coriander

½ tsp ground cardamom

1 tsp ground oregano

3 large cloves garlic, crushed

1 medium onion, thinly sliced

4 sprigs thyme

1½ tsp (8 g) fine sea salt, or to taste

2 8-rib frenched racks of lamb (3 lb [1.4 kg]), separated

Naan, soft pita, or tortilla, for serving

Red onion, finely sliced, for topping

Cilantro, for topping

Lime juice, for topping

Add the orange juice, lime juice, vinegar, olive oil, pimentón, 7 spice, cumin, coriander, cardamom, oregano, garlic, onion, thyme, and salt to a bowl and mix together until well combined. Place the lamb in a ziplock bag and pour the sauce over it. Let the lamb sit in the marinade for at least 3 hours or overnight in the refrigerator. Bring the meat to room temperature before cooking, about 90 minutes after removing it from the refrigerator.

(continued)

For the Chipotle Sauce

1 or 2 chipotle chiles in adobo, depending on desired level of heat

1 tsp dried oregano

3 cloves garlic

1 medium tomato

½ medium onion

½ cup (10 g) cilantro

¼ cup (60 ml) lime juice

1 tbsp (15 ml) apple cider vinegar

⅛ tsp fine sea salt

Yogurt Sauce

½ cup (115 g) plain yogurt

2 tbsp (32 g) tahini

2 tbsp (30 ml) lemon juice

1 large clove garlic, finely minced

⅛ tsp salt

Prepare the chipotle sauce by combining the chipotle chiles, oregano, garlic, tomato, onion, cilantro, lime juice, vinegar, and salt in a food processor or blender. Pulse everything until smooth, taste for seasoning, and set aside.

For the yogurt sauce, add the plain yogurt, tahini, lemon juice, garlic, and salt to a small bowl and whisk together until smooth.

Place a large skillet, preferably cast iron, over medium-high heat. Once it becomes hot, shake the marinade off the lamb pieces and place them in the pan. Be sure to not overcrowd the pan, so that the meat has enough space to sear. Cook the lamb until it is browned on each side, 3 to 4 minutes. Remove it at this point for medium-rare meat or reduce the heat to medium-low and continue to cook to your preferred level of doneness. Place the lamb in a dish, cover with aluminum foil, and leave it to rest for 10 minutes. Then remove the meat from the bone and chop.

Arrange the lamb on the soft naan with the chipotle sauce and yogurt sauce. Top with sliced onion, cilantro, and fresh lime juice.

Note: *Feel free to reduce the ingredients in this recipe significantly by rubbing the lamb chops with spices and seasoning and not using liquids or aromatics for a marinade.*

Moussaka–Layered Eggplant, Potato, and Meat Dish

Serves 4–6

2 medium eggplants, sliced into vertical ½" (1-cm)-wide strips or rounds

6 tbsp (90 ml) extra-virgin olive oil, divided

2¾ tsp (14 g) fine sea salt, divided

1 large onion, finely chopped

4 large cloves garlic, finely minced

Freshly ground black pepper

1 tsp 7 spice

1 tsp ground cumin

½ tsp ground cardamom

1⅓ lb (600 g) ground beef, lamb, or a combination of both

2 tbsp (42 g) pomegranate molasses

2 tbsp (32 g) tomato paste

1 tbsp (15 g) sweet chili sauce or shatta

2 large tomatoes, peeled and diced

½ cup (10 g) fresh parsley

4 large Idaho potatoes, cubed

2 tbsp (28 g) salted butter

¼ cup (60 ml) whole milk or water

Moussaka *literally means "chilled" in Arabic. It is also the name of this dish, which consists of layered eggplant, meat, and potato. Traditionally, similar eggplant recipes would be chilled and then served cold. It is the shepherd's pie of the eastern Mediterranean and is popular in Greece, Egypt, and the Levant. This recipe is not difficult, only slightly lengthy. It requires some multitasking, but the result will be sure to impress. The juicy layers of eggplant and meat taste divine alongside the creamy potatoes. The recipe's generous quantity and savory nature make this dish the ultimate family-style meal.*

Preheat the oven to 425°F (220°C) and place the eggplant pieces on a baking sheet. Prick them with a fork and brush with 3 tablespoons (45 ml) of olive oil. Season the eggplant with 1 teaspoon of salt and bake for 30 minutes, flipping halfway through.

In the meantime, add 3 tablespoons (45 ml) of olive oil to a pan. Set the heat to medium, stir in the onion, and cook it for about 10 minutes, or until soft and transparent. Add the garlic, pepper, 7 spice, cumin, and cardamom and cook for another 2 minutes. Then stir in the meat, ¾ teaspoon of salt, pomegranate molasses, tomato paste, and chili sauce. Stir the ingredients together and cook for 5 minutes. Stir in the tomatoes and parsley, cover the pan, and reduce the heat to low. Cook for about 20 minutes, or until the tomatoes have dissolved. Taste for seasoning and set aside.

Place the potatoes in a medium pot filled with boiling water and 1 teaspoon of salt. Set the heat to high and simmer the potatoes for about 15 minutes, or until tender. Drain the potatoes, add the freshly ground black pepper, butter, and milk, and mash until smooth. Taste for seasoning and set aside.

Begin arranging the layers in a 13 x 9–inch (33 x 23–cm) casserole dish. Lightly grease the pan with olive oil and assemble the eggplant on the bottom of the pan to cover it. Then, add the meat sauce. Spoon dollops of the potatoes over the meat and use the bottom of a spoon to gently smooth it out. Set the pan aside while you prepare the béchamel sauce.

(continued)

For the Béchamel Sauce

3 tbsp (42 g) salted butter

3 tbsp (33 g) all-purpose flour

2 cups (480 ml) whole milk

½ tsp fine sea salt, or more if omitting parmesan

Freshly ground pepper

⅛ tsp ground nutmeg

½ cup (45 g) grated parmesan, or more to taste, optional

Turn the oven broiler on low. Combine the butter and flour in a saucepan and set it over medium-high heat. Whisk the mixture constantly until it turns a sandy color, 4 to 5 minutes. Whisk in the milk and continue to beat until the sauce has thickened, another 5 minutes or so. Reduce the heat if the sauce begins to foam up. Stir in the salt, pepper, nutmeg, and parmesan, if desired, and remove the pot from the heat. Pour the sauce over the potatoes and place the pot in the oven under a low broiler. Keep an eye on the moussaka and remove it after 5 to 10 minutes, or after it has some golden spots over the surface. Allow the pie to cool for at least 10 minutes before serving.

Sweet and Sticky Lamb Chops with Apricots, Orange Blossom, and Shallots

Serves 4

8 lamb chops (1½–2 lb [680–910 g]), fatty parts trimmed

1 tsp fine sea salt plus a pinch, divided

Freshly ground black pepper

2 tbsp (30 ml) extra-virgin olive oil

3 tbsp (45 ml) balsamic vinegar

1 cup (240 ml) fresh orange juice

2 sprigs thyme

1 sprig rosemary

5 large cloves garlic, sliced

4 shallots or ½ a medium onion, very finely sliced

5 dried apricots, finely diced

2 tbsp (42 g) orange blossom honey

Aleppo chili flakes, for topping

Fresh mint and parsley, chopped, for topping

These sweet and sticky lamb chops are so simple to put together on a busy weeknight. I like to use orange juice and honey infused with thyme for a simple yet succulent sauce. Serve with a vibrant salad such as the Chickpea, Bulgur, and Citrus Salad (page 90) or rice pilaf (page 114).

Season the lamb with 1 teaspoon of salt and pepper 1 hour before cooking. Place a grill pan or skillet over medium-high heat, add the olive oil, and wait for it to heat thoroughly. Place the lamb chops in the pan, cooking for 3 minutes on one side and 2 minutes on the other. The lamb chops should develop a golden-brown crust on both sides. Remove the lamb chops from the heat and place them onto a serving plate.

In a small bowl, mix together the balsamic, orange juice, thyme, and rosemary. Pour the mixture into a saucepan, stir in the garlic, shallots, dried apricots, and a pinch of salt, and bring to a simmer over medium heat. Simmer for about 10 minutes and then stir in the honey. Drizzle the sauce over the lamb chops and top with chili flakes and chopped mint and parsley.

Braised Lamb Shanks with Tamarind

Tamarind is used in Levantine dishes such as meat-stuffed carrots simmered in tomato sauce. It imparts a sweet, sour, and slightly bitter profile to sauces. But a little tamarind goes a long way, so if you want to add more, taste as you go. Tamarind paste gives this braising sauce a vibrant tang. Like the vinegar, it also serves to tenderize the lamb. Prepare to fill your home with the aroma of comfort.

Serves 4

2 tsp (10 g) fine sea salt

Freshly ground black pepper

5 cloves garlic

2 tsp (6 g) 7 spice

2 tsp (6 g) ground cumin

2 tsp (6 g) ground coriander

1 tsp ground cardamom

½ tsp ground cinnamon

4 medium lamb shanks, excess fat trimmed

¼ cup (60 ml) extra-virgin olive oil, divided

1 medium onion, finely diced

1 red pepper, finely diced

2 large carrots, finely diced

2 ribs celery, finely diced

3 bay leaves

5 cups (1.2 L) hot vegetable stock

3 tbsp (48 g) tomato paste

2 tbsp (30 ml) apple cider vinegar

2 tbsp (42 g) honey

2 tbsp (42 g) tamarind paste

6 thyme sprigs

Preheat the oven to 325°F (160°C). Add the salt, pepper, garlic, 7 spice, cumin, coriander, cardamom, and cinnamon to a small bowl and mix together to combine. Place the lamb shanks in a large bowl and add the spice mixture. Rub the meat with the spices until thoroughly covered. Set the lamb aside for 30 minutes at room temperature before searing it. If the meat is coming straight out of the refrigerator, let it come to room temperature before putting it on the heat. This should take about 90 minutes.

Place a large oven-proof pot, preferably a Dutch oven, over medium-high heat. When the pot is hot, add 2 tablespoons (30 ml) of olive oil and add the meat. Sear it on both sides until it has a deep brown color, about 3 minutes per side. Remove the lamb from the pot and set aside. Add another 2 tablespoons (30 ml) of oil to the pot, reduce the heat to medium, and stir in the onion, red pepper, carrots, celery, and bay leaves. Sauté the vegetables for about 10 minutes, stirring often. Add the hot stock, tomato paste, vinegar, honey, tamarind, and thyme. Stir everything together and bring the pot to a simmer. Add the lamb shanks and place the pot in the oven, uncovered. Roast for about 3 hours, while basting the meat with the juices every 30 minutes.

Remove the bay leaves. Serve the lamb shanks with the braising liquid.

Spice Routes: Lamb almost always goes hand in hand with 7 spice (for more on 7 spice, see Spices, page 158) in the eastern Mediterranean. The spice blend is warm, sweet, and aromatic. It is a natural partner to the tart tamarind sauce in this recipe. Cardamom adds a fresh, floral layer to the meat, washing away any gaminess.

Stuffed Eggplants

Serves 4

This is one of my favorite dishes. It is so simple to put together and full of flavor. Different versions of eggplants stuffed with lamb are enjoyed throughout the Mediterranean. Sheikh el mahshi in the Levant or papoutsakia in Greece are just a few examples. Serve the stuffed eggplant with a side of white rice or salad. Or as I often prefer, combine all of the aubergine flesh with the cooked lamb and serve on warm naan with yogurt and fresh herbs. You cannot go wrong.

2 medium eggplants, vertically halved

5 tbsp (75 ml) extra-virgin olive oil, divided

1¼ tsp (7 g) fine sea salt, divided

Freshly ground black pepper

1 large onion, finely chopped

1 jarred roasted red pepper, chopped

1 lb (450 g) ground lamb

1 tsp 7 spice

1 tsp pimentón dulce

1 tsp ground cumin

2 tbsp (42 g) pomegranate molasses

1 cup (240 g) strained tomatoes or passata

3 tsp (15 g) sweet chili sauce or shatta

3 large cloves garlic, crushed

½ cup (10 g) cilantro, chopped

Fresh parsley, for topping

Pine nuts, toasted, for topping

Rice, for serving

Salad, for serving

Warm bread, for serving

Preheat the oven to 425°F (220°C). Prick the halved eggplants with a fork and brush the surfaces with 2 tablespoons (30 ml) of olive oil. Season them with ¼ teaspoon of salt and a good grinding of freshly ground black pepper. Place the eggplants skin side down on a baking sheet and bake for 35 to 40 minutes, or until golden brown.

Add 3 tablespoons (45 ml) of olive oil to a large pan or pot. Sauté the onion over medium-low heat for 15 minutes, stirring often. Add the red pepper, lamb, 7 spice, pimentón dulce, and cumin and cook until browned. Then add the pomegranate molasses, strained tomatoes, chili sauce, garlic, cilantro, 1 teaspoon of salt or to taste, and freshly ground black pepper. Stir the meat sauce and bring it to a simmer. Cover the pan, reduce the heat to low, and cook for 20 minutes, stirring occasionally.

Scoop out about two-thirds of the eggplant flesh and mix with the meat sauce. Then, spoon the sauce into the wells of the eggplant. Top with fresh parsley and toasted pine nuts and serve with rice, salad, or warm bread.

Chimichurri Steak

Serves 4

1½ lb (680 g) flank steak (see Tip)

1⅛ tsp (7 g) fine sea salt

Freshly ground black pepper

Sweet chili sauce or shatta, for serving

For the Green Chimichurri

½ medium onion or 2 shallots, chopped

1 red jalapeño, seeds and rinds removed

6 cloves garlic

¼ cup (60 ml) apple cider vinegar

¼ cup (60 ml) lime juice

1 cup (25 g) fresh flat leaf parsley

½ cup (10 g) cilantro, plus more for serving

½ cup (20 g) mint leaves

2 tbsp (6 g) fresh oregano

½ cup (120 ml) extra-virgin olive oil

They say that the word "chimichurri" comes from a Basque word tximitxurri, meaning "a mixture of many things." Chimichurri is an Argentinian steak recipe, but its use of ingredients is all too similar to those of the western and eastern Mediterranean. I used flank steak here, which I hammered slightly to make it more even. However, feel free to use any long cut of steak you prefer. The marinade helps to tenderize even the toughest cuts.

Season the steak with 1⅛ teaspoons of fine sea salt and a good grinding of black pepper. If the meat is coming straight out of the refrigerator, keep it out at room temperature for 90 minutes before putting it on the heat. This will allow the meat to brown better and cook more evenly.

Place all of the chimichurri ingredients in a food processor and pulse until smooth. Place half of the green marinade in a ziplock bag or bowl with the steak and toss to coat them in the sauce. Seal the bag or bowl tightly and let the steak marinate in the refrigerator for at least 4 hours or overnight. Place the rest of the chimichurri sauce in an airtight container and store in the refrigerator until you prepare the steak.

Place a griddle pan or cast-iron pan over medium-high heat and place the steak inside, shaking off the excess marinade before putting it on the heat. Sear the steak for about 4 minutes on each side. Then reduce the heat to low and continue to cook the steak for another 6 to 10 minutes depending on your preferred level of doneness. A meat thermometer is helpful in cooking the meat just the way you want. Insert it into the center of the thickest part of the meat. Remove the meat from the heat at 120°F (50°C) for rare, 130°F (50°C) for medium rare, 140°F (60°C) for medium, 150°F (70°C) for medium-well, and 160°F (70°C) for well-done. Place the steak in a serving dish, cover, and let it rest for 10 minutes.

Season the reserved sauce with a generous pinch of salt and spoon it over the steak along with chili sauce and cilantro.

Tip: *If the steak is not even in thickness, use a meat hammer to flatten it so that it is about ¾ inch (2 cm) thick so it will cook evenly.*

Roasted Chicken Thighs with Preserved Lemon, Dates, and Honey

Serves 4

1 preserved lemon

3 tbsp (45 ml) extra-virgin olive oil

¼ cup (60 ml) lemon juice

1½ tsp fine sea salt

1 large onion, finely sliced

8 large cloves garlic, peeled and lightly crushed

1 tsp ground cumin

1 tsp 7 spice

½ tsp ground cinnamon

1 tbsp (6 g) coriander seeds, crushed

Freshly ground pepper

⅛ tsp cayenne pepper

2 tbsp (42 g) orange blossom honey

6 large Medjoul dates, pits removed, coarsely chopped

4–6 chicken thighs (2½ lb [1.1 kg])

Fresh cilantro, chopped, for topping

Both preserved lemons and plenty of lemon juice add a burst of sunshine to this dish. The marinade works with any cut of chicken you prefer, and it is especially delicious for a whole roasted chicken. I use chicken thighs in this recipe, which take little time to cook and are succulent, tender, and juicy with the sauce. Serve with roasted baby potatoes or a fresh salad.

Remove and discard the pulp of the preserved lemon and finely dice it. Place it in a bowl along with the olive oil, lemon juice, salt, onion, garlic, cumin, 7 spice, cinnamon, coriander, pepper, cayenne, and honey. Mix everything together until well combined. Pour the marinade into a large ziplock bag, add the dates and chicken, seal the bag, and rub the chicken with the sauce. Refrigerate for at least 4 hours or preferably overnight. Let the chicken come to room temperature, about 90 minutes, before roasting it.

Preheat the oven to 400°F (200°C). Place the chicken and all the contents of the ziplock bag onto a large baking or roasting tray and roast the chicken for 40 to 45 minutes, or until golden brown, basting it with the sauce every 15 minutes or so. The internal temperature should register at least 165°F (70°C).

Serve with any sauces from the pan alongside the date pieces and fresh cilantro.

Spice Routes: The warmth and nuttiness of coriander complements the citrusy flavors and the sweetness of the dates in this roast. Crush the whole spice with a mortar and pestle to release its natural oils and aroma before using.

Roasted Chicken with Pomegranate Glaze and Sumac

Serves 4

4 whole chicken legs (3½ lb [1.6 kg])

2 tsp (10 g) fine sea salt

Freshly ground black pepper

1 cup (240 ml) pomegranate juice

¼ cup (80 g) pomegranate molasses

2 tbsp (32 g) tomato paste

3 tbsp (45 ml) extra-virgin olive oil

¼ cup (60 ml) lemon juice

1 tbsp (12 g) sumac spice, plus more for topping

4 large cloves garlic, finely chopped

4 sprigs fresh thyme

1 large red onion, thinly sliced

Pomegranate seeds, for topping

Fresh parsley, for topping

This recipe has been a readers' favorite on my blog for many years now. Inspired by the Levantine fall, it is characterized by tangy and tart pomegranate and vibrant lemon. I make this when the colors begin to fade away outside and I need a lift. This roast is perfect served with a vibrant salad or a creamy freekeh risotto. It is my definition of feel-good food.

Rub the chicken with salt and pepper and set aside. Add the pomegranate juice, molasses, tomato paste, olive oil, lemon juice, and sumac to a bowl and whisk to combine. Pour the mixture into a large ziplock bag and add the chicken, garlic, thyme, and onion. Seal the bag, massage everything together, and let the chicken marinate in the sauce for at least 4 hours or overnight.

Preheat the oven to 400°F (200°C). Then arrange the chicken pieces in a roasting dish or baking tray and pour the marinade inside. Roast for 45 to 50 minutes depending on the size of the pieces, or until the chicken has a rich golden color and is cooked to your liking. Baste the chicken with the sauce every 15 minutes while it is in the oven. When done, it should register at least 165°F (70°C) when a meat thermometer is inserted into the thickest part of the chicken.

Serve the chicken with fresh pomegranate seeds and parsley.

Pan-Fried Seeded Chicken Fillet

Serves 4

4 boneless, skinless chicken breasts (3 lb [1.4 kg]), halved and pounded to ¼" (6-mm) thickness

1 tsp fine sea salt, divided

Freshly ground black pepper

2 tsp (6 g) ground cumin

2 tsp (6 g) ground coriander

⅛ tsp cayenne

1 tsp granulated garlic

2 tbsp (6 g) dried thyme

2 tbsp (6 g) dried mint

1 tsp Aleppo chili flakes

2 tbsp (20 g) toasted sesame seeds

1 cup (80 g) panko

¼ cup (5 g) parsley

¼ cup (5 g) basil leaves

½ cup (60 g) all-purpose flour

2 large eggs

Extra-virgin olive oil, for panfrying

These succulent chicken breasts are coated in spices and herbs and then pan-fried in olive oil. The result is tender, juicy, homestyle chicken that is perfect for everyday meals. A true comfort dish. Serve alongside a citrusy green salad or creamy potatoes.

Preheat the oven to 400°F (200°C). Place a large piece of plastic wrap onto a kitchen surface. Arrange the chicken breasts on top and then cover with another piece of plastic wrap. Pound the chicken so that it is about ¼ inch (6 mm) thick and set it aside. Enjoy this therapeutic moment in the kitchen and release any tension you may have had in your day.

Combine ½ teaspoon of salt, the pepper, cumin, coriander, cayenne, and garlic in a small bowl. Rub the chicken with the spice mixture and set it aside. In a large bowl, add the thyme, mint, chili, sesame seeds, panko, parsley, basil, and ½ teaspoon of salt. Mix and set aside. Place the flour in another dish. And lastly, beat the eggs in a separate bowl. Lightly coat the chicken with the flour, then dip it into the egg, and coat with the crumb mixture.

Place a large skillet over medium heat and add 4 tablespoons (60 ml) of olive oil. When the oil starts to sizzle when some crumbs are dropped inside, add the chicken pieces, about three pieces at a time. Panfry for about 4 minutes on each side, or until golden. Remove the chicken from the heat and add a splash of more oil if necessary. Heat the oil before repeating the process with the rest of the chicken. Transfer the cooked chicken onto a baking sheet and bake for 8 to 10 minutes, or until it is cooked through.

Musakhan Salad

Serves 4

Musakhan is a Palestinian village dish that consists of juicy roasted chicken and caramelized onions infused with sumac and then served on fluffy taboon bread. It is one of my favorite dishes of all time, but a bit heavy for everyday meals. For that reason, I thought of giving the recipe a lighter twist full of the flavors that make the dish so mouthwatering. Salad is a deceptive word for this recipe, as it is both satisfying and indulgent. Pita croutons infused with olive oil and sumac, express pickled red onion, and deeply spiced chicken make this dish hit home.

For the Chicken

2 tsp (6 g) 7 spice

1 tsp ground coriander

1 tsp ground cumin

½ tsp ground cardamom

1½ tsp (8 g) fine sea salt

Freshly ground black pepper

2 tbsp (20 g) sumac

¼ cup (60 ml) lemon juice

3 tbsp (45 ml) extra-virgin olive oil

8 boneless, skinless chicken thighs (about 2 lb [910 g])

1 large onion, finely sliced

For the Salad

2 medium pita breads, cut into about 1" (2.5-cm) squares

6 tbsp (90 ml) extra-virgin olive oil, divided

4 tbsp (40 g) sumac, divided

1 large red onion, finely sliced

¼ cup (60 ml) fresh lemon juice

1 medium bunch romaine lettuce, chopped

½ cup (90 g) pomegranate seeds

2 stalks green onion, sliced

Handful of mint leaves, finely chopped

Handful of parsley, finely chopped

2 tbsp (42 g) pomegranate molasses

2 large cloves garlic, finely minced

1 tsp fine sea salt

2 tbsp (20 g) toasted pine nuts, for topping

Combine the 7 spice, coriander, cumin, cardamom, salt, pepper, sumac, lemon juice, and olive oil in a small bowl and whisk. Pour the sauce into a ziplock bag and add the chicken thighs and onion. Let the chicken marinate in the sauce for at least 4 hours or overnight.

For the salad, start by making the pita croutons. Preheat the oven to 425°F (220°C) and place the cut pita bread on a large baking tray. Add 2 tablespoons (30 ml) of olive oil and toss to coat the bread. Bake the bread for about 6 minutes, remove from the oven and stir in 2 tablespoons (20 g) of sumac. Bake for another 4 to 6 minutes, or until the bread is crisp. Keep an eye on the oven so that the sumac does not burn.

Reduce the oven heat to 400°F (200°C). Arrange the marinated chicken in a large baking dish and pour the juices and onion over the top. Roast the chicken for about 40 minutes, or until tender. Discard the onion, set the chicken aside to cool slightly, and then slice the chicken into strips.

Place the red onion and lemon juice in a small bowl, toss to combine, and set it aside for at least 10 minutes. This will soften the flavor of the onion. Place the romaine lettuce, pomegranate seeds, green onion, mint, and parsley in a serving bowl and combine. In a small bowl, mix together the pomegranate molasses, garlic, salt, 2 tablespoons (20 g) of sumac, and 4 tablespoons (60 ml) of olive oil. Stir the red onion and its juices into the pomegranate dressing and toss the mixture with the salad. Add the chicken pieces and pita croutons and top with toasted pine nuts. Enjoy at once!

Fruits of the Sea

When one thinks of the Mediterranean, the smell of the ocean often comes to mind. The region does, after all, get its name from the waters that border it—the Mediterranean Sea. From the coastal cities of Valencia and Santorini to Beirut and Jaffa, culinary traditions are shaped by coastal living. The enjoyment of fish and seafood is often centered around slowing down the rhythm of life and living in the moment.

The lifestyle is characterized by the fruits of the sea. In many coastal areas, at least one day of the week is reserved for a seafood feast. Fish and seafood are often celebrated by being enjoyed moderately, sustainably, and seasonally. Sea bass, monkfish, swordfish, mullet, tuna, sardines, halibut, anchovies, mussels, clams, prawns, shrimp, squid, and flounder are all plentiful in the region. And there is an abundance of ways to serve and enjoy them. From grilling and roasting to ancient preservation techniques such as ceviche or escabeche, the options are limitless.

Fish and seafood are best enjoyed simply, so that the flavor of the ocean is really appreciated. Less is more when it comes to cooking fish. Less cooking time, less spices, and less condiments result in better taste and texture. The key to good fish is retaining moisture, so the shortest cooking time possible is ideal. Herbs and aromatics, however, are always a plus.

One of the things that I love about maritime delights is how little time is required to produce delicious, exciting, and satisfying dishes. In this chapter, you will find many meals that come together in 30 minutes or less. Fideuá, seafood stews, and ceviche are all festive, yet undemanding—making for more time to enjoy with guests. Because that is the essence of the Mediterranean way. The joy in cooking and eating is centered on the people we share those moments with.

Fish and Seafood Stew with Preserved Lemon

Serves 4

While the recipes in this book all come from my personal notebook, this is the one that my family and friends know as being the most intimate. It is perfect for winter and summer alike, but I prefer it in the former—because it brings people together. Perfect for cozying up, a warm stew on a chilly day is guaranteed to keep the winter blues away. The fish and seafood are simmered in a heartwarming tomato stew infused with plenty of nostalgia-inducing aromatics. The dish never fails to remind me of my childhood summers in Jaffa, an ancient Canaanite port city on the Mediterranean Sea. Characterized by fragrant saffron and flavorful preserved lemon, this stew is full of life and joy. Serve with crisp, warm bread for dunking or a side of fluffy white rice. And most importantly, enjoy with your favorite people.

3 tbsp (45 ml) extra-virgin olive oil

1 medium onion, finely diced

1 medium carrot, finely diced

2 ribs celery, finely diced

½ red bell pepper, finely diced

3 large cloves garlic, finely minced

3 anchovies, finely chopped

1 preserved lemon, finely chopped

Pinch of Iranian or Spanish saffron (about 20 threads)

½ tsp pimentón dulce or sweet paprika

Dash of cayenne pepper

½ tsp ground cumin

3 tbsp (48 g) tomato paste

5 pitted Spanish manzanilla olives, jarred variety

3 medium tomatoes, coarsely chopped

3 cups (720 ml) homemade seafood stock or water (see Notes, page 82)

½ tsp fine sea salt

Freshly ground black pepper

2 medium cod fillets or other white fish of choice, cut into chunks

16 jumbo shrimp, peeled and deveined

12 mussels, scrubbed, beards removed

¼ cup (60 ml) fresh lemon juice

Fresh parsley, for topping

Place a large pot over medium heat and add the olive oil. Stir in the onion, carrot, celery, and red pepper. Sauté the vegetables for 10 to 12 minutes. Add the garlic, anchovies, preserved lemon, saffron, pimentón dulce, cayenne, and cumin. Sauté for another 3 minutes. Then, add the tomato paste and olives and continue cooking for another few minutes. Stir in the tomatoes and home-made seafood stock. Add just enough liquid to cover the ingredients.

Adjust the thickness of the stew to your liking as it simmers by adding more or less stock. Season with salt and pepper, cover, reduce the heat to medium-low, and leave to simmer until the tomatoes become tender and fall apart, about 15 minutes.

Add the fish chunks and cook for another 10 minutes. Then add the shrimp and mussels and simmer for 8 to 10 minutes. Discard any unopened mussels. Taste the stew for salt, and adjust to your liking. Bear in mind the saltiness of the anchovies, preserved lemon, fish, and seafood.

Stir the lemon juice into the stew, top with parsley, and serve with warm, fluffy rice or bread.

Spice Routes: Spanish seafood stews make plentiful use of saffron and pimentón dulce. Moroccan stews would be incomplete without preserved lemon. The vibes of this dish are reminiscent of Tangier, the cultural cross-roads between southern Spain and Morocco. Considering that these are neighboring cuisines, it's not surprising that the combination of flavors works splendidly here.

Spiced Lemon and Basil Calamari

Serves 4

1 lb (450 g) squid tubes, cleaned and cut into ½" (1-cm) rings

¾ cup (180 ml) milk

1 large egg

8 fresh basil leaves, chopped

1 tsp freshly grated lemon zest

2 cups (250 g) all-purpose flour

1 tsp pimentón dulce

½ tsp ground cumin

½ tsp Aleppo chili flakes

1½ tsp (8 g) fine sea salt

Freshly ground black pepper

Canola oil, for frying

Coarse sea salt, for topping

Lemon, cut into wedges, for serving

Aioli, for serving

The concepts of mezze, tapas, and antipasti have always been prevalent in my upbringing. Whether in Spain or the Levant, these dishes were made for socializing, breaking the ice, sparking conversation, and of course, fueling our appetites. This Spanish-style calamari fritter recipe is an essential in my home, both for entertaining and casual dinners. The combination of lemon, basil, cumin, and pimentón dulce really elevates this popular tapa. Serve with saffron aioli.

Pat the squid dry with paper towels. Whisk together the milk, egg, basil, and lemon zest until smooth. Put the calamari in the milk mixture, cover, and place it in the refrigerator for 30 minutes.

Place the flour, pimentón dulce, cumin, and chili flakes in a large bowl. Season generously with salt and pepper and mix together. Coat the calamari in the flour mixture and place it in a dish. Fill a large, heavy-based pot with at least 2 inches (5 cm) of oil and turn the heat to medium-high or heat the oil until it reaches 375°F (190°C). Fry the squid for about 2 minutes, or until golden. Spoon the calamari from the pot, shaking off any excess oil, and place it on a large dish lined with a paper towel. Serve topped with coarse sea salt and lemon wedges to squeeze lemon juice as desired. Enjoy on its own or with aioli.

Note: *This cheat aioli recipe is great when you are pressed for time: Soak 3 large crushed cloves of garlic and a small pinch of saffron in 3 tablespoons (45 ml) of lemon juice for 10 minutes. Then, stir the mixture into 6 tablespoons (90 g) of good-quality mayonnaise and season with sea salt.*

Spice Routes: Cumin and pimentón dulce are essential pairings with seafood. Their earthy qualities balance the flavors of the sea.

Mediterranean White Fish with Herb Sauce

Serves 4

This is my favorite way to roast white fish. It is one of the most flavorful ways to enjoy it. The inside of the fish is filled with aromatics and the outside is coated in an herby and lemony green sauce. Prepare yourself for a burst of flavors. Use the freshest fish you can find. If it smells like the sea, take it. If it smells too fishy, look elsewhere.

For the Fish

4 whole snapper or seabass (6–8 lb [2.7–3.6 kg]), cleaned and scaled, sliced halfway from the bottom up

4 tbsp (60 ml) extra-virgin olive oil, plus more for topping

2 tsp (6 g) pimentón dulce or sweet paprika

1 tsp ground cumin

1 tsp ground coriander

2 tsp (10 g) fine sea salt

Freshly ground black pepper

4 large cloves garlic, finely minced

2 jalapeño peppers, seeds and rinds removed, finely sliced, plus more for topping

4 cilantro stems

4 tsp (20 g) sweet chili sauce, shatta, or harissa

2 lemons, finely sliced, plus 1 more for topping

Fresh lemon juice

Parsley, for topping

For the Herb Sauce

½ cup (10 g) cilantro

1 large clove garlic

⅛ tsp salt

¼ cup (60 ml) lime juice

¼ cup (60 ml) olive oil

Ask your fishmonger to clean and cut the fish for you. If you buy whole snapper or sea bass, use a sharp knife to slice the fish halfway from the bottoms up. Make three incisions across both sides of the fish.

Preheat the oven to 400°F (200°C) and line a large baking sheet with aluminum foil. Arrange the fish pieces on the sheet and drizzle with olive oil throughout the inside and outside of the fish, using a tablespoon (15 ml) of oil for each fish. Season the inside and outside of each fish with ½ teaspoon of pimentón, ¼ teaspoon of cumin, ¼ teaspoon of coriander, ½ teaspoon of sea salt, and freshly ground black pepper. Focus on the inside of the fish when seasoning while sprinkling the surface with salt and spices as well. Rub the spices and seasonings on the fish to spread thoroughly. Stuff each fish with 1 clove of minced garlic, a quarter of the sliced jalapeño, 1 stem of cilantro, 1 teaspoon of chili sauce, and lemon slices, reserving one lemon for topping.

Squeeze lemon juice onto the surfaces of the fish, cover loosely with aluminum foil, and bake for 20 minutes. Then remove the aluminum and bake for another 25 to 30 minutes, or until the fish is fully cooked through.

For the herb sauce, add the cilantro, garlic, salt, lime juice, and olive oil to a food processor and blend until smooth. Set aside until serving the fish.

Spread the herb sauce on the cooked fish and serve with fresh lemon.

Tahini and Honey-Poached Salmon

Serves 4

⅓ cup (70 g) tahini paste

⅓ cup (80 ml) lemon juice (juice of about 2 large lemons)

1 tbsp (21 g) honey

1¼ tsp fine sea salt, divided

⅓ cup (80 ml) water

4 salmon fillets (20–24 oz [570–680 g])

Freshly ground black pepper

5 tbsp (75 ml) extra-virgin olive oil, divided

1 large onion, finely sliced

3 large cloves garlic, finely minced

½ tsp ground cumin

For Garnish

Pomegranate seeds

Pine nuts, toasted

Fresh parsley, finely chopped

Pomegranate molasses

Tahini and fish almost always go together in the Levant. However, an uncooked tahini sauce is usually served alongside other mezze dishes on the final table. I like to simmer tahini and honey, which quickly reduce into a delicious sauce. While I used to poach the salmon in the sauce, I now prefer to sear it to get a nice crispy, golden crust. This is a simple dish that will leave a lasting impression.

Mix the tahini, lemon juice, honey, ¼ teaspoon of salt and water until smooth and set aside. Season each salmon fillet with ¼ teaspoon of salt and freshly ground black pepper. Place a large skillet over medium-high heat and add 2 tablespoons (30 ml) of olive oil. When the oil is hot, place the salmon pieces, skin side up, in the pan. Cook the fish for 3 minutes, reduce the heat to medium, gently flip the salmon, and cook it for another 4 minutes. Remove it from the heat and set it aside.

Add 3 tablespoons (45 ml) of olive oil to the pan and stir in the onion. Reduce the heat to medium-low and cook for 10 to 12 minutes, stirring often. Add the garlic and cumin and cook for another 2 minutes. Stir in the prepared tahini sauce and simmer for 5 minutes. Arrange the salmon fillets on the sauce and cook for another minute or two. Serve with pomegranate seeds, pine nuts, parsley, and pomegranate molasses.

Ceviche

Serves 4

½ cup (120 ml) lime juice

¼ cup (60 ml) orange juice

1 tbsp (15 ml) apple cider vinegar

1 tbsp (21 g) honey

1 lb (450 g) skinless halibut, seabass, or flounder fillets, cut into ½–¾" (1–2-cm) cubes

½ large red onion, finely sliced

Handful of cilantro, finely chopped

Handful of parsley, finely chopped

1 medium green jalapeño, seeds and membranes removed, finely diced

15 heirloom cherry tomatoes, quartered

1 medium cucumber, peeled and diced

½ medium red bell pepper, finely diced

1 avocado, diced

2 large cloves garlic, finely minced

5 manzanilla olives, chopped

2 tbsp (30 ml) extra-virgin olive oil

1 tsp fine sea salt, or to taste

Freshly ground black pepper

2 tsp (8 g) ground sumac

Aleppo chili flakes, for topping

Crisp pita chips, for serving

Before the advent of refrigerators or iceboxes, ancient preservation techniques such as ceviche and escabeche were used to make fish, seafood, and meats last longer. Like escabeche, the idea of ceviche is "cooking" raw fish with acid. Citrus such as orange juice and lime juice combined with vinegar cure the fish, making it both safe and delicious to eat. You will notice the fish harden and lighten in color, appearing cooked after about 40 minutes in the refrigerator. It will continue to cure as time passes, so keep your eye on it so that it does not "overcook" and become too chewy. Get the freshest white fish you can find. Ceviche works well with halibut, grouper, seabass, flounder, and mahi-mahi.

Place the lime juice, orange juice, vinegar, and honey in a small bowl and whisk together until well combined. Place the fish in a deep dish or medium bowl and pour the marinade on top to cover it. Cover the dish with plastic wrap and let the fish marinate in the refrigerator for 1 to 2 hours. Give the fish a stir after 30 minutes and adjust the marinating time to your taste. I prefer to serve the fish after 1 hour for a soft and tender center. It will become chewier and less tender after 90 minutes.

Combine the onion, cilantro, parsley, jalapeño, cherry tomatoes, cucumber, red pepper, avocado, garlic, and olives in a serving dish. Stir in the olive oil, marinated fish, and a few tablespoons (45 ml) of its juices. Season the ceviche with salt, pepper, and sumac. Top with chili flakes. Serve right away with crisp pita chips.

Couscous alla Trapanese – Sicilian Fish and Semolina Stew

Serves 4

Vivid images of the breezy Sicilian seaside come to mind. The smell of the sea is a reminder of a shared ocean and not-so-distant cultures. Much of Sicilian cuisine has a prominent North African influence, mostly of Tunisian and Algerian origins. The name of this dish says it all—couscous alla Trapanese, or "Trapani-style couscous." Common Middle Eastern ingredients such as pine nuts, cinnamon, almonds, raisins, and saffron all became staples in Sicilian cuisine during the Middle Ages, a golden time for the expansion of the culinary world. This dish is intensely flavorful and full of life. My version differs slightly from the traditional one, as I add extra spices and aromatics.

Begin by preparing the tomato broth. Place a medium pot or deep pan over medium heat. Add the olive oil and stir in the onion, carrot, celery, and red pepper. Stir in ⅛ teaspoon of salt and sauté for about 10 minutes, or until the onion is soft and transparent. Add the pimentón dulce and cumin and cook for another 2 minutes. Stir in the garlic, preserved lemon, tomatoes, tomato paste, stock, ½ teaspoon of salt, and pepper.

Cover the pot, reduce the heat to low, and simmer the sauce for 25 minutes. Gently stir in the fish and cook for another 10 minutes. Add the shellfish and cook for another 8 minutes. If you are using mussels, discard any that have remained unopened.

(continued)

For the Broth

3 tbsp (45 ml) extra-virgin olive oil

½ large onion

1 medium carrot, finely diced

2 ribs celery, finely chopped

½ large red pepper, finely chopped

⅝ tsp fine sea salt, divided

1 tsp pimentón dulce

½ tsp cumin

3 large cloves garlic, crushed

1 preserved lemon

4 tomatoes, peeled and chopped

2 tbsp (32 g) tomato paste

1 cup (240 ml) homemade seafood stock, vegetable stock, or water (see Notes, page 82)

Freshly ground black pepper

1 lb (450 g) halibut fish fillet, cut into cubes

1 lb (450 g) shellfish such as shrimp, calamari, and mussels, cleaned

For the Couscous

2 tbsp (30 ml) extra-virgin olive oil

1 tbsp (14 g) salted butter

½ large onion, finely chopped

2 cinnamon sticks

2 tbsp (40 g) golden raisins

2 bay leaves

Pinch of saffron (about 20 threads), soaked in hot water or milk

2½ cups (600 ml) vegetable stock, homemade seafood stock, or water (see Notes, page 82)

1 tsp fine sea salt

2 cups (320 g) good-quality hand-rolled couscous

For Garnish

Slivered almonds and/or pine nuts, toasted

Fresh parsley

Aleppo chili flakes

Lemon wedges

Meanwhile, prepare the couscous. Place a large pot over medium heat. Add olive oil and butter and stir in the onion, cinnamon sticks, raisins, and bay leaves. Sauté for 10 to 12 minutes, stirring often. Add the saffron, stock, and salt. Bring the liquid to a boil and stir in the couscous. Remove the pot from the heat, cover with a tight-fitting lid, and let the couscous steam for 5 minutes, or until the seafood and tomato broth is ready. Fluff the couscous with a fork after it is ready. Remove the bay leaves and cinnamon sticks.

Transfer the couscous to a serving dish and spoon the fish and seafood over the top along with some of its broth to your taste. Serve the broth separately to wet the couscous as you like. Top the couscous with toasted almonds and/or pine nuts, parsley, and chili flakes. Serve with plenty of lemon. And most importantly, savor the moment.

Fideuá–Seafood and Fish Noodles with Preserved Lemon

Serves 4

6 tbsp (90 ml), extra-virgin olive oil, divided

2 cups (200 g) vermicelli noodles (see Notes)

1 lb (450 g) red king prawns or jumbo shrimp, deveined, with shells and tails left intact (see Notes)

2 cleaned squid tubes with tentacles, chopped

1 large onion, finely chopped

3 large cloves garlic, finely minced

2 tomatoes, finely chopped

1 tbsp (16 g) tomato paste

1 preserved lemon, rinsed and finely diced

½ tsp ground cinnamon

½ tsp ground cumin

1 tsp pimentón dulce or sweet paprika

⅛ tsp cayenne pepper, or to taste

Pinch of saffron (20–30 threads), soaked in 2 tbsp (30 ml) hot water

1 tsp fine sea salt, or to taste

½ lb (230 g) monkfish fillet, cod, or hake, cubed

4–5 cups (1–1.2 L) homemade seafood, chicken, or vegetable stock (see Notes)

This is a Valencian dish with ingredients of Middle Eastern origins, and it is my favorite seafood recipe in the book. The combination of toasted vermicelli, saffron, cumin, and cinnamon tells stories of a bygone era. The preserved lemon is the perfect addition, contributing plenty of gusto that marries so well with the flavors of the sea. I like the final dish brothy, or caldoso/melosito, as is said in Spanish— almost like a noodle stew. The key to a good fideuá, like a flavorful paella, is using a good broth and stir-frying the base ingredients until golden and fragrant.

Place a large pan or paella pan over medium heat and add 2 tablespoons (30 ml) of olive oil. Panfry the vermicelli for about 3 minutes, or until lightly golden, stirring often. Remove the noodles from the pan and set them aside.

Increase the temperature to medium-high and add another 2 tablespoons (30 ml) of olive oil. When the oil is hot, panfry the prawn until lightly golden, for about 2 minutes on each side. Remove them from the heat and set aside.

Add yet another 2 tablespoons (30 ml) of oil to the pan and stir-fry the squid over high heat until golden. Reduce the heat to medium-low and stir in the onion. Continue cooking while stirring until soft and transparent, about 10 minutes. Stir in the garlic and cook for another 2 minutes. Add the tomatoes, tomato paste, preserved lemon, cinnamon, cumin, pimentón dulce, cayenne, saffron, and salt. Gently stir in the fish pieces and 4 cups (960 ml) of broth, cover the pan, reduce the heat to medium-low, and let the sauce simmer for 20 minutes.

(continued)

Spice Routes: One of the key ingredients in this fideuá, aside from saffron, pimentón, and cumin, is cinnamon, which gives the dish a sweet and warm flavor. Use Ceylon cinnamon if you can find it, as it is sweeter and less intense than cassia.

10 mussels

Fresh parsley, chopped, plus more for topping

Lemon wedges, for serving

Stir in the fried vermicelli and parsley and cook for 8 minutes, or until the noodles are al dente, stirring occasionally and tasting for salt. Add more broth as needed to keep the noodles wet. Arrange the prawn and mussels on top, cover the pan and cook for another 6 to 8 minutes. The noodles should be loose and there should still be some broth. If necessary, add more liquid to reach this consistency, being careful not to overcook the noodles. Top with fresh parsley and serve right away with plenty of fresh lemon.

Notes: *To make your own seafood stock beforehand, simmer 1 medium onion, a pinch of saffron, fish, shrimp, fine sea salt, and fish bones in 5 cups (1.2 L) of water for 30 minutes. Strain the solids out of the broth. If you're short on time, an express option is using an organic chicken stock cube dissolved in hot water.*

If you are using angel hair pasta or capellini instead of vermicelli, break the pasta into 1-inch (2.5-cm) pieces.

You can use any seafood medley you prefer. Shrimp, prawns, mussels, squid, and fish are the popular ones.

The unpeeled prawns or shrimp are mostly for aesthetic purposes and look great when entertaining, so feel free to use peeled and deveined shrimp with the tails left intact for more casual meals.

Mussels Escabeche

Serves 4 as a starter

½ lemon, finely sliced

½ tsp fine sea salt

2 lb (910 g) mussels, scrubbed, beards removed

½ cup (120 ml) extra-virgin olive oil

½ medium onion, finely diced

1 medium carrot, finely diced

3 thyme sprigs

5 large cloves garlic, finely minced

2 bay leaves

1 cinnamon stick

1 tsp pimentón dulce

2 tbsp (30 ml) rice vinegar

1 tbsp (21 g) honey

¼ cup (60 ml) fresh lemon juice

2 tbsp (5 g) fresh parsley

¼ tsp Aleppo chili flakes

Bread, for serving

Pasta, for serving

The concept of food conservation or preservation with vinegar or sugar was introduced by the Moors in southern Spain. The technique not only preserves food but intensifies its flavors. Older methods from the 13th century relied on high amounts of vinegar to preserve fish or seafood for long periods of time. Given that times have evolved, so have the amounts of acids needed in recipes like these. I love this escabeche served with warm bread or tossed in angel hair pasta. Traditionally, the escabeche is stored in an airtight container and kept in the fridge for 2 to 3 days before serving, resulting in a more pickled, vinegary flavor. However, I prefer to enjoy it warm and straight out of the pan.

Place a large pan over medium heat and add the lemon, salt, and 1 cup (240 ml) of boiling water. Bring the water down to a simmer. Add the mussels, reduce the heat to low, cover the pan, and cook for 6 to 8 minutes, or until the shells have opened. Leave the lid just slightly open if the liquid begins to foam up. Discard any mussels that remain unopened and set the rest of the mussels aside to cool. Separate the mussel meat from the shells, discard the shells and lemon, and set aside.

Rinse the pan and place it over medium heat. Add the olive oil and stir in the onion, carrot, and thyme. Cook for 12 minutes, stirring often, until the onion is soft. Add the garlic, bay leaves, cinnamon, and pimentón and cook for another 5 minutes. Stir in the vinegar, bring to a simmer, and cook for another 5 minutes. Add the honey and lemon juice and stir to combine. Remove the bay leaves and cinnamon stick, then toss the mussels into the vegetable mixture. Add the parsley and chili flakes. Serve right away or refrigerate overnight or for up to 3 days. Serve with bread or tossed in pasta.

Sweet and Sour Tamarind Shrimp

Serves 4

¼ cup (60 ml) extra-virgin olive oil

½ cup (120 ml) lemon juice, plus more for topping

6 large cloves garlic, finely minced

3 tsp (22 g) tamarind paste

2 tbsp (32 g) tomato paste

2 tbsp (42 g) honey

Handful of parsley, finely chopped, plus more for topping

½ tsp fine sea salt

Freshly ground pepper

20 raw jumbo shrimp or prawns (1 lb [450 g]), deveined with shells and tails left intact

This sweet, sour, and sticky tamarind sauce will leave you craving more. The tanginess of the tamarind pairs perfectly with the delicate flavor of the shrimp. Be careful to use tamarind in small amounts, as too much will overpower a dish. The sauce also works divinely for other fish marinades and is ideal for barbecues. I prefer to use tamarind paste, as it is ready to use, as opposed to tamarind concentrate.

Place the olive oil, lemon juice, garlic, tamarind, tomato paste, honey, parsley, salt, and pepper in a bowl and mix together to combine. Toss the shrimp in the sauce, cover, and let it marinate in the refrigerator for 30 minutes.

Place a griddle pan over medium-high heat. Arrange the shrimp on skewers, 5 shrimp per skewer, and grill for 2 to 3 minutes on each side, or until the shrimp is cooked through Brush the shrimp with the leftover marinade while it is on the heat for more flavor. Serve with fresh parsley and lemon juice.

Vibrant Vegetables

The Mediterranean lifestyle is all about seasonal eating. Fresh produce is sought out from local farmers and meals are often served from ground to plate. When vegetables are at their peak, they taste better. They are both more delicious and more nutritious. In October, nothing compares to the flavor of freshly squeezed olive oil with the perfect balance of fruitiness and piquancy. Or crisp greens that burst with flavor in the spring. I will never forget the first time that I had melt-in-your-mouth Medjoul dates right after their harvest. I learned to appreciate waiting for the right time to get the most out of produce.

Below is a guide, generally relevant to the Northern Hemisphere, for enjoying Mediterranean fruits and vegetables while they are in season. Be familiar with the seasons for your local harvests to get the most out of your produce. Because all good things take time.

Spring: artichokes, asparagus, wild greens, spinach, za'atar or wild thyme, cabbage, radishes, fennel, strawberries, dates, and stone fruit such as loquats, cherries, and apricots

Summer: tomatoes, grapes and grape leaves, cactus pears, zucchini, eggplants, cucumbers, purslane, dandelion greens, corn, peaches, nectarines, and plums

Fall: olives, figs, pomegranates, carob, persimmon, pumpkin, squash, sweet potatoes, and quince

Winter: lemons, oranges, pomelos, clementines, potatoes, carrots, rutabaga, turnips, and cabbage

Chickpea, Bulgur, and Citrus Salad

Serves 4

¼ cup (38 g) fine bulgur wheat

⅓ cup (80 ml) fresh orange juice,

1 tsp orange zest (about ½ orange)

2 tbsp (30 ml) fresh lemon juice

2 tbsp (30 ml) extra-virgin olive oil

1 tbsp (21 g) honey

½ tsp fine sea salt

2 medium cucumbers, diced

2 medium tomatoes, diced

1 cup (160 g) cooked or canned garbanzos

½ cup (20 g) fresh mint, chopped

½ cup (10 g) parsley, finely chopped

4 tbsp (60 g) sultanas or golden raisins

2 tbsp (30 g) pistachio nuts, coarsely chopped

2 tbsp (30 g) slivered almonds, toasted

This is a delicious summer salad with chickpeas (aka garbanzo beans) that can be enjoyed all year long. It is perfect in the winter when we are craving a little sunshine. The flavors are fresh, citrusy, and oh so satisfying. This particular salad takes me to Tunis, where citrus grows in abundance. I like serving this salad with lamb dishes. But on more casual days, a side of panfried halloumi is more than welcome.

Combine the bulgur and ⅓ cup (80 ml) of boiling water in a small bowl. Cover the bowl with plastic wrap and let it steam for 10 minutes. Place the orange juice, orange zest, lemon juice, olive oil, honey, and salt in a small bowl and mix together until the dressing is emulsified. Set it aside.

Place the cucumbers, tomatoes, garbanzos, mint, parsley, sultanas, pistachios, and almonds in a serving bowl and toss together. Stir in the prepared bulgur and citrus dressing and toss again. Taste for seasoning.

Mushroom, Bulgur, and Herb "Meatballs" with Tahini

Serves 4

This recipe was born after some of my lovely readers requested traditional Levantine recipes made meat-free. I thought that the combination of mushrooms and lentils make a delicious substitute for the traditional kofta. These "meatballs" are divine with a citrusy tahini sauce and fresh herbs. Serve with fluffy white rice or inside warm pita bread.

For the Meatballs

¼ cup (38 g) fine bulgur wheat

10 baby bella mushrooms, coarsely chopped

3 tbsp (45 ml) extra-virgin olive oil, divided

2 cups (480 ml) vegetable stock

1 cup (180 g) green lentils, soaked in water for 30 minutes and drained

1½ tsp fine sea salt, divided

1 large egg or egg substitute, beaten

½ cup (10 g) parsley, plus more for topping

½ cup (10 g) cilantro

3 stalks green onion, coarsely chopped

1 tsp 7 spice

1 tsp ground cumin

Freshly ground black pepper

½ tsp Aleppo chili flakes, plus more for topping

Pine nuts, toasted, for topping

For the Tahini Sauce

½ cup (120 g) tahini paste

½ cup (120 ml) fresh lemon juice

⅔ cup (160 ml) water

Pinch of fine sea salt, or to taste

2 large cloves garlic, finely minced

Dash of cayenne pepper

Combine the bulgur with ¼ cup (60 ml) of boiling water, cover, and let it steam for 5 minutes.

Sauté the mushrooms in a large pan over medium heat with 2 tablespoons (30 ml) of olive oil. Cook them for about 6 minutes, or until golden and tender. Remove the mushrooms from the heat and set aside.

Place a medium pot over high heat and pour in the vegetable stock. Add the lentils and ½ teaspoon of salt. Cover the pot, reduce the heat to low, and simmer for 20 minutes. Place the lentils in a colander to remove any extra water. Excess liquid in the meatballs will cause them to fall apart.

Preheat the oven to 400°F (200°C). Place the lentils in a food processor and add the cooked mushrooms, egg, parsley, cilantro, green onion, 7 spice, cumin, 1 teaspoon of salt, pepper, and chili. Pulse until the mixture comes together.

Lightly grease a baking dish with olive oil and shape the mushroom and lentil mixture into about 1-tablespoon (15-ml)-sized balls. Arrange them in the pan and bake for about 15 minutes. They should be firm and keep their shape.

In the meantime, mix the tahini sauce ingredients until smooth. When the meatballs are ready, top with the sauce, and place under a high broil just until the sauce gets a few golden spots. Top with fresh parsley, chili flakes, and toasted pine nuts.

Mixed Green, Risoni, and Strawberry Salad

Serves 4

¾ tsp fine sea salt, or to taste, plus more for pasta water

⅔ cup (113 g) risoni or orzo pasta

3 tbsp (45 ml) extra-virgin olive oil, divided

4 cups (120 g) mixed greens (arugula and/or baby spinach)

3 radishes, finely sliced

8 large strawberries, quartered

1 cup (150 g) seedless red grapes, halved

½ cup (90 g) pomegranate seeds

3 tbsp (21 g) sliced almonds, toasted

2 tbsp (42 g) pomegranate molasses

1 tbsp (15 ml) apple cider vinegar

2 tbsp (30 ml) lemon juice

2 tsp (8 g) poppy seeds

Freshly ground black pepper

This is a delicious winter/spring salad that celebrates the produce of the seasons. I often make this around February or March, when the winter begins to overstay its welcome. Sometimes I substitute beetroot for the grapes. This is also a delicious option if you do not mind staining your pasta. Because we eat with our eyes first.

Bring a medium pot of water to a boil, season it generously with salt, and cook the risoni according to the package instructions. Be sure to remove it from the heat while it still has a bite, or while the texture is al dente. Drain the pasta, stir in a tablespoon (15 ml) of olive oil, and set it aside to cool.

Combine the risoni, greens, radishes, strawberries, grapes, pomegranate seeds, and almonds in a salad bowl.

Mix together the pomegranate molasses, vinegar, 2 tablespoons (30 ml) of olive oil, lemon juice, poppy seeds, salt, and pepper. Pour the dressing over the salad bowl and toss to combine.

Roasted Cauliflower and Eggplant with Dukkah and Chili

Serves 4

1 medium eggplant, cut into 1" (2.5-cm) cubes

1 small–medium cauliflower, cut into florets

6 tbsp (90 ml) extra-virgin olive oil, divided

½ tsp ground turmeric

1 tsp ground cumin, divided

1¼ tsp (7 g) fine sea salt, divided

Freshly ground black pepper

4 large cloves garlic, crushed, divided

Dukkah, for topping

For the Herb Sauce

½ cup (10 g) cilantro

½ cup (10 g) fresh parsley

1 mild green chili such as jalapeño, seeds removed

2 tbsp (30 ml) lime juice

Generous pinch of Aleppo chili flakes

3 tbsp (45 ml) extra-virgin olive oil

Pinch of salt

For the Tahini Sauce

¼ cup (60 g) tahini

¼ cup (60 ml) lemon juice

2 tbsp (30 ml) water

Pinch of salt

This dish is perfect for the late fall, when we crave all things roasted. It is one of my favorite ways to enjoy cauliflower and a recipe that gets made time and time again in my kitchen. It can be served as a side, but I find it more than satisfying on its own.

Preheat the oven to 400°F (200°C). Line two separate baking sheets with parchment paper. Add the eggplant to one tray and the cauliflower to the other. Toss the eggplant with 2 tablespoons (30 ml) of olive oil and the cauliflower with 4 tablespoons (60 ml) of oil. Season and toss the cauliflower with all of the turmeric, ½ teaspoon of cumin, ¾ teaspoon of salt, pepper, and 2 crushed cloves of garlic. Season and toss the eggplant with ½ teaspoon of cumin, ½ teaspoon of salt, black pepper, and another 2 crushed cloves of garlic. Bake the vegetables for 30 minutes, or until golden, tossing them halfway through.

In the meantime, for the herb sauce, place the cilantro, parsley, green chili, lime juice, chili flakes, olive oil, and salt in a food processor. Pulse the mixture until smooth and set aside.

Combine all of the tahini sauce ingredients and set aside until serving.

Combine the cauliflower and eggplant in a serving dish. Top with the herb sauce and tahini sauce. Sprinkle dukkah over the top and serve.

Spice Routes: Dukkah is an Egyptian spice mix made of nuts, spices, and seeds. It originated in ancient Egypt due to its strategic location between the spice routes. The nuts and spices used in it may be adjusted to your taste. You may use almonds or cashews in place of hazelnuts, for example. Dukkah's citrusy and nutty notes pair well with tahini.

Canaanite Tomato and Pomegranate Salad

Serves 4

1 pita bread, cut into 1" (2.5-cm) squares

5 tbsp (75 ml) extra-virgin olive oil, divided

Pinch plus ¾ tsp fine sea salt, divided

2 tbsp (20 g) za'atar

4 tbsp (60 ml) fresh lemon juice

2 tbsp (42 g) pomegranate molasses

2 tsp (8 g) ground sumac

Freshly ground black pepper

4 cups (600 g) heirloom cherry tomatoes, halved

1 cup (170 g) pomegranate seeds

1 medium red bell pepper, chopped into 1" (2.5-cm) squares

1 bunch fresh parsley, finely chopped

½ cup (20 g) fresh mint leaves

½ cup (10 g) fresh basil leaves

2 stalks green onion, finely sliced

2 tbsp (20 g) pine nuts, toasted

1 cup (160 g) cubed feta cheese or farmer's cheese

This take on fattoush salad celebrates late summer tomatoes and early fall pomegranates. The za'atar and olive oil–infused pita crisps add a lovely crunch that pairs perfectly with the fresh fruit and vegetables. Use a fruity and slightly peppery olive oil for another layer of depth.

Preheat the oven to 400°F (200°C) and toss the pita bread with 2 tablespoons (30 ml) of olive oil and a pinch of salt. Spread the bread onto a large baking sheet and bake for about 6 minutes. Remove it from the oven and toss the bread with the za'atar. Put it back into the oven and bake for another 5 to 6 minutes, or until crisp. Keep your eye on the za'atar so that it doesn't burn. Set the pita crisps aside.

Place 3 tablespoons (45 ml) of olive oil, lemon juice, pomegranate molasses, sumac, ¾ teaspoon of salt, and pepper in a small bowl. Mix the dressing until well combined, check for seasoning, and set aside.

Add the tomatoes, pomegranate seeds, red pepper, parsley, mint, basil, green onion, pine nuts, and feta to a salad bowl and gently toss together. Add the dressing and toss another time. Serve with the pita crisps.

Purslane, Sun-Dried Tomato, and Fig Salad

Serves 4

½ medium red onion, finely sliced

¼ cup (60 ml) fresh lemon juice

Pinch plus ¾ tsp fine sea salt, divided

1 tbsp (15 ml) balsamic vinegar

2 tbsp (40 g) fig jam

2 tbsp (30 ml) extra-virgin olive oil

Freshly ground black pepper

1 tsp orange zest (about ½ orange)

4 cups (80 g) purslane, baby arugula, or a combination of both

½ cup (100 g) sun-dried tomatoes

6 figs, quartered

1 large orange, peeled and segmented

½ cup (60 g) walnuts, toasted and chopped

½ cup (80 g) crumbled feta cheese

This is another wonderful autumnal salad. Golden sunsets, cool breezes, and figs as sweet as candy are just a few of my favorite things about the season. Purslane, which has often been discarded as a useless weed, is quite popular in Levantine cuisine. It is delicious, tangy, and chock-full of flavor. You may find some at your local's farmer's market. If not, the next most similar greens would be baby arugula and baby spinach.

Place the onion, lemon juice, and pinch of salt in a bowl and toss to combine. Set it aside for 10 minutes before adding it to the salad. This will reduce the onion's pungency.

Add the balsamic vinegar, fig jam, olive oil, ¾ teaspoon of salt, pepper, and orange zest to a small bowl and whisk together to emulsify. Set aside.

Combine the purslane, sun-dried tomatoes, figs, orange, walnuts, feta, and the onion and its juices in a serving bowl. Drizzle the vinaigrette over the salad and toss to combine. Serve right away.

Artichoke and Cannellini Paella

Serves 4

¼ cup (60 ml) extra-virgin olive oil, plus more for topping

1 large yellow onion, finely chopped

2 medium jarred roasted red peppers, finely chopped (see Notes)

1 large carrot, finely chopped

Pinch plus 2 tsp (10 g) fine sea salt, divided

Freshly ground black pepper

3 anchovies, finely chopped, optional

5 large cloves garlic, finely minced

1 bay leaf

5 pitted manzanilla olives

3 medium tomatoes, diced

1 tsp pimentón dulce

½ tsp ground cumin

½ tsp fennel seeds

Pinch of saffron (about 20 threads), soaked in 2 tbsp (30 ml) boiling water

2 cups (240 g) frozen artichoke hearts, thawed

1½ cups (300 g) paella rice such as Bomba, not rinsed

4 cups (960 ml) low-sodium vegetable stock

½ cup (10 g) packed cilantro, finely chopped

1½ cups (130 g) cannellini beans, cooked or canned, drained

½ cup (10 g) fresh parsley, finely chopped, for topping

¼ cup (60 ml) fresh lemon juice, for topping

Aleppo chili flakes, for topping

Lemon wedges, for serving

This is in all honesty my favorite kind of paella. It is hearty, exploding with flavor, and nourishing for the soul. The artichoke and cannellini make it both savory and rich. The result is a paella that is vibrant and festive, making it perfect for serving crowds. Its flavors are further enhanced by saffron, pimentón dulce, and roasted red pepper. The paella rice is typically left with a bite, but add about another 5 minutes of cooking time if you prefer it softer.

Heat the olive oil in a large, shallow pan or paella pan—I use a 13-inch (33-cm) pan—over medium heat. Stir in the onion, red peppers, carrot, a generous pinch of salt, and pepper. Sauté the base vegetables for about 10 minutes, stirring often. Stir in the anchovies if desired, garlic, bay leaf, olives, tomatoes, pimentón dulce, cumin, fennel, saffron, and artichoke, and simmer for another 5 minutes.

Then stir in the rice, cook for 3 minutes, and add the stock, 2 teaspoons (10 g) of salt, and freshly ground black pepper. Stir the rice occasionally during the next 10 minutes and then add the cilantro and cannellini beans. Stir gently for 5 minutes, reduce the heat to low, cover the pan, and cook for another 10 minutes or so. Add liquid as needed to keep the rice moist. It will take 22 to 25 minutes total, depending on how much of a bite you want in the grain. Remove the bay leaf. Top with fresh parsley, lemon juice, olive oil, chili flakes, and lemon wedges. Serve at once!

Notes: *Mushrooms and asparagus are also delicious vegetable options for this style of paella.*

Feel free to substitute a fresh red bell pepper for the jarred roasted red pepper.

Summer Nights Watermelon, Cheese, Fig, and Mint Salad

Serves 4

½ cup (65 g) pistachio nuts

1 tbsp (13 g) granulated sugar

3 tbsp (45 ml) extra-virgin olive oil

1 tbsp (21 g) orange blossom honey

4 cups (600 g) cubed watermelon

8 medium figs, quartered

½ cup (20 g) fresh mint leaves

8 oz (230 g) semi-creamy feta cheese

Flaky sea salt, for topping

When summer meets fall, the most amazing thing happens—watermelon and figs are both in season for a brief period of time. And in my kitchen that means that this salad is happening, almost every other evening. It is a joy to eat, representing the Mediterranean way of living—fresh, vibrant, and colorful. Like many of the best things in life, simple is best.

Place a medium nonstick skillet over medium heat. Add the pistachios and sugar and toss together to combine. Stir them together until the sugar dissolves and the nuts are golden, 3 to 4 minutes. Place the pistachios on a piece of parchment paper and let them cool.

Mix together the olive oil and honey and set aside. Place the watermelon, figs, mint, and feta in a serving bowl and gently toss together. Drizzle the olive oil–honey dressing over the top and scatter the candied nuts and flaky salt. Enjoy right away.

Green Eggs

Serves 2

3 tbsp (45 ml) extra-virgin olive oil

2 medium leeks, white and light green parts, finely sliced

1 medium green chili, seeds removed

Pinch plus ⅓ tsp fine sea salt, divided, plus more to taste

2 large cloves garlic, finely minced

1 cup (185 g) butterbeans

1½ cups (45 g) fresh watercress

¼ cup (5 g) cilantro

Handful of mint

1½ cups (360 ml) vegetable stock or water

Freshly ground black pepper

4 large free-range eggs

2 stalks green onion, sliced, for topping

Aleppo chili flakes, for topping

Za'atar, for topping

Crumbled feta, for topping

Warm bread, for serving

This is one of my versions of shakshuka, a North African dish consisting of eggs poached in a hearty tomato sauce. The green concoction adds a sense of mystery, but the flavors are as fresh as it gets. Watercress may seem too pungent for some, but it completely mellows down after cooking. The butterbeans also serve to add creaminess to a bright and tangy sauce. Serve with warm, crispy sourdough bread for dipping.

Heat the olive oil in a pan over medium heat. Add the leeks, chili, and a pinch of salt and sauté for 8 to 10 minutes. Stir in the garlic, beans, watercress, cilantro, and mint. Cook for another 5 minutes. Add 1 cup (240 ml) of vegetable stock, ⅓ teaspoon of salt, and black pepper, and bring to a simmer. Transfer everything to a blender and pulse until smooth. Pour the liquid back into the pan. Use a spoon to make a well, crack an egg inside, and repeat with the rest of the eggs. Season with salt and pepper and cook for 5 to 7 minutes, or until the eggs are done to your taste. Cover them during the last minute or two to cook the tops. Top with fresh green onion, chili flakes, za'atar, and feta. Enjoy with warm bread.

Grains

Throughout history, wheat has been seen as sustenance itself. To this day, bread is known as *eish* in Egypt, meaning "life." Grains are the most consumed food in the world, serving to feed the planet's 7.6 billion people. Every society has a preferred grain that they serve alongside main dishes.

In the eastern Mediterranean, or the lands covering the original fertile crescent, rice and wheat are enjoyed in a plentitude of ways. From bulgur to farro to freekeh, types and methods of harvesting, roasting, and cooking wheat have been around since ancient times. Recently, however, many of these grains have resurfaced. They can be cooked in sophisticated, exciting, and modern ways. Freekeh, for example, which has traditionally been cooked as a stew or pilaf, is also delicious cooked risotto-style. I love a creamy freekeh in Baked Portobello Mushrooms Stuffed with Freekeh (page 39). A Bulgur Pilaf (page 110) is a versatile side dish to serve alongside a variety of meat, poultry, and fish mains. Farro (page 113), like most of the grains enjoyed throughout the Mediterranean, has been around since ancient times. Its neutral taste, however, allows for limitless flavor combinations.

While I wish I could cover the abundance of grains in the region and my favorite methods of cooking them, I will simply share some essential bulgur, rice, and farro dishes, along with a few of my favorite pies. They are perfect for pairing with the main recipes in this book.

Bulgur Pilaf

Serves 4

This bulgur pilaf is my go-to recipe for serving alongside meat or fish recipes, such as my Roasted Chicken with Pomegranate Glaze and Sumac (page 61). But more often than not, I will double the herbs and enjoy it with roasted eggplant and yogurt. The flavors are fresh, vibrant, and homey.

3 tbsp (45 ml) extra-virgin olive oil

1 medium onion

Pinch plus 1¾ tsp (9 g) fine sea salt, divided

3 large cloves garlic, finely minced

1½ cups (260 g) coarse bulgur wheat

3 cups (720 ml) hot vegetable stock

Freshly ground black pepper

1 bay leaf

¼ tsp turmeric

1 cup (25 g) fresh parsley

1 cup (20 g) cilantro

½ cup (20 g) fresh mint

½ cup (90 g) pomegranate seeds

3 tbsp (30 g) sultanas or golden raisins

¼ cup (60 ml) fresh lemon juice

Olive oil, for topping

Slivered almonds, toasted, for topping

Pine nuts, toasted, for topping

Place a medium pot over medium heat and add the olive oil. Stir in the onion, add a pinch of salt, and sauté it for about 12 minutes. Stir in the garlic and cook for another 2 minutes. Add the bulgur and toast it for 5 minutes.

Pour in the hot stock and add 1¾ teaspoons of salt, pepper, bay leaf, and turmeric. Stir everything together, cover the pot, and reduce the heat to low. Cook the bulgur for 15 to 20 minutes, or until tender to the bite. Remove the bay leaf. Spoon the bulgur into a serving dish and stir in the parsley, cilantro, mint, pomegranate, sultanas, and lemon juice. Serve with a drizzle of olive oil, almonds, and pine nuts.

Mushroom, Fava Bean, and Farro Pilaf

Serves 4

6 tbsp (90 g) extra-virgin olive oil, divided

2 leeks white and light green parts, chopped

Pinch plus 1½ tsp (8 g) fine sea salt, divided

1½ cups (250 g) farro

1 tbsp (14 g) unsalted butter

Freshly ground black pepper

4 large cloves garlic, crushed, divided

1 bay leaf

4 cups (960 ml) vegetable stock

2 cups (240 g) fava beans, peeled, thawed if from frozen (see Note)

1 lb (450 g) baby bella mushrooms

⅓ cup (33 g) grated parmesan

1 cup (25 g) packed fresh parsley, finely chopped

Farro is a Mediterranean superfood and ancient grain. It is literally whole wheat. And in the Levant, the same is known as kameh, *or simply "wheat." Farro is tender and has a wholesome and mild taste that pairs well with mushrooms and legumes. This grain is as simple to cook as it is delicious.*

Add 3 tablespoons (45 ml) of olive oil to a medium pot placed over medium heat. Stir in the leeks, add a pinch of salt, and cook them for about 8 minutes. Stir in the farro and toast the grain for 3 minutes. Add 1 tablespoon (14 g) of butter, 1 teaspoon of salt, a good grinding of black pepper, 2 cloves of crushed garlic, the bay leaf, and the stock. Bring the pot to a boil, reduce the heat to low, cover, and simmer for 20 minutes, or until the farro is tender to the bite. Remove the bay leaf.

In another pan, heat 2 tablespoons (30 ml) of olive oil and stir in 2 cloves of crushed garlic and ¼ teaspoon of salt. Sauté the fava beans for 5 to 7 minutes, or until lightly golden. Set aside.

Add another tablespoon (15 ml) of oil to the pan and toss in the mushrooms to coat. Cook them for about 6 minutes over medium-high heat, or until golden. Then season the mushrooms with ¼ teaspoon of salt and set aside.

Combine the farro, fava beans, and mushrooms in a serving bowl and toss with the grated parmesan and parsley.

> Note: *You may find frozen peeled fava beans at your local Middle Eastern or international food store.*

Black or Wild Rice Pilaf with Sweet Potato and Herbs

Serves 4

2 tbsp (30 ml) extra-virgin olive oil

3 sweet potatoes, cubed

1¼ tsp (7 g) fine sea salt, divided

Freshly ground black pepper

3½ cups (840 ml) vegetable broth or water

1½ cups (280 g) black rice

1 bay leaf

⅓ cinnamon stick

4 cardamom pods, lightly crushed

1 cup (25 g) packed parsley, finely chopped

2 stalks green onion, finely sliced

1 tsp pomegranate molasses, for topping

½ cup (90 g) pomegranate seeds

3 tbsp (10 g) pumpkin seeds, toasted

3 tbsp (30 g) sultanas or golden raisins

3 tbsp (21 g) almond slices, toasted, for topping

1 tbsp (15 ml) olive oil, for topping

This is another ancient grain that is still relatively uncommon in everyday cooking. It was known as "forbidden rice" during ancient times in China. This was because only royalty could afford to enjoy it. Black rice is deeply nutty, rich, and satisfying. Its flavor pairs well with autumn produce such as sweet potato, pumpkin, and squash. I like to cook it with cinnamon and cardamom as well. The rice is delicious alongside roasted chicken, such as the Roasted Chicken Thighs with Preserved Lemon, Dates, and Honey (page 58) or white fish.

Preheat the oven to 425°F (220°C) and add the olive oil to a large baking tray. Toss the sweet potatoes in the oil with ½ teaspoon of salt and freshly ground black pepper. Bake for about 25 minutes, tossing the potatoes halfway through.

Heat a medium pot and add the broth. Bring it to a boil and stir in the rice, ¾ teaspoon of salt, bay leaf, cinnamon, and cardamom. Cover the pot, reduce the heat to low, and simmer the rice for about 35 minutes, or until tender, but with a bite. Remove the rice from the heat and keep it covered for another 10 minutes. Remove the bay leaf and cinnamon stick. Fluff it with a fork before serving.

Combine the rice and sweet potatoes in a serving bowl and toss with the parsley, green onion, pomegranate molasses and seeds, pumpkin, and sultanas. Top with toasted almonds and olive oil.

Fragrant Orange Blossom, Herb, and Pistachio Basmati

Serves 4–6

3 tbsp (45 g) sultanas or golden raisins

2 cinnamon sticks

6 cloves cardamom lightly crushed

3 cloves

1 bay leaf

2¼ tsp plus a pinch (11 g) fine sea salt, divided

1½ cups (280 g) basmati rice, well rinsed

2 tbsp (32 g) vegetable ghee

2 tbsp (28 g) salted butter

1 medium onion, finely diced

3 large cloves garlic, finely minced

2 tsp (6 g) cumin seeds, lightly crushed

Pinch of saffron (about 20 threads), soaked in 2 tbsp (30 ml) hot water

1 tsp orange blossom water

¼ cup (38 g) unsalted pistachio nuts, toasted

5 dried apricots, chopped

2 tbsp (20 g) currants

½ cup (10 g) parsley, finely chopped

½ cup (10 g) cilantro, finely chopped

This pilaf is so aromatic that you may just spend more time smelling it than eating it. The scents of deep spices and fresh orange blossom will take you places. The pilaf method is an excellent way of capturing the flavors and aromas that you are infusing your food with. It also results in perfectly fluffy and tender grains.

Rice was so important in the royal kitchens of the Levant during the Middle Ages that chefs would be tested solely on how well they made it. This simple recipe, however, is anything but intimidating. The most important part is making sure that the rice still has a bite to it before draining it. The result will be a foolproof, fluffy, and fragrant pilaf.

Add 8 cups (1.9 L) of hot water to a medium pot and bring to a boil. Stir in the sultanas, cinnamon, cardamom, cloves, bay leaf and 2 teaspoons (10 g) of salt. Stir the rice into the pot and simmer over medium-high heat for 7 to 8 minutes—it should still have a bite to it. Drain the rice and set it aside.

Meanwhile, heat the ghee and butter in another pot and stir in the onion with a pinch of salt. Bring the heat to medium and sauté the onion for about 15 minutes. Then add the garlic, cumin seeds, saffron and its liquid, and ¼ teaspoon of salt. Cook for another 2 minutes. Stir in the orange blossom water and then the rice, and cook for another 2 minutes while stirring often. Remove the pot from the heat, tightly cover it, and let the rice steam for 10 minutes. Add the pistachios, apricots, currants, parsley, and cilantro and toss with a fork to combine. Remove the bay leaf and cinnamon stick. Enjoy right away.

Tomato, Onion, and Za'atar Tart

Serves 4–6

3 tbsp (45 ml) extra-virgin olive oil

1 large yellow onion, finely sliced

⅛ tsp fine sea salt, plus more for sprinkling

Freshly ground black pepper

1 (8.5-oz [245-g]) sheet puff pastry, thawed

1 tbsp (9 g) all-purpose flour

1 tbsp (10 g) za'atar, plus more for topping

2 tbsp (30 g) pesto (see Note)

4.3 oz (120 g) buffalo mozzarella, cut into 8 (⅛" [3-mm]-thick) slices

10 cherry or grape tomatoes, sliced in half

1 medium tomato, finely sliced

1 large egg, beaten with 1 tbsp (15 ml) water

Fresh basil, for topping

This summer-style tart is basically a combination of my favorite things: caramelized onions, sweet and juicy seasonal tomatoes, fresh pesto, za'atar, and cheese. Need I say more? The caramelized onion is an important component of this recipe in terms of flavor. You could put caramelized onion on plain bread and it would taste delicious, if you ask me. You may use a pie crust or short crust pastry for this pie, as I often do. But given that I like to make this on lazy days, ready puff pastry is my preferred route for express baking. One may be tempted to fill the tart with tomatoes, but they will release too much liquid during baking, making for a soggy bottom. Slice them finely and you will get a pie that is both beautiful and crisp. Reduce the amount of oil that goes on the dough as much as you can to keep it from absorbing too much moisture.

Heat a skillet over medium-low heat and add the olive oil, the sliced onion, ⅛ teaspoon of salt, and pepper. Cook, stirring often, for 35 to 40 minutes, or until the onion is sweet and caramelized. Remove it from the heat and set aside.

Preheat the oven to 400°F (200°C) and line a baking sheet with parchment paper. Place the pastry dough on the tray and flatten it so that it is about 12 × 9 inches (30 × 23 cm) and ⅛ inch (3 mm) thick. Top the surface of the dough with the flour and za'atar, leaving a 1-inch (2.5-cm) border. Then, spread a thin layer of pesto within the same borders. Add 3 tablespoons (45 g) of the caramelized onion and then layer it with the mozzarella slices. Finally, arrange the tomatoes on top, sprinkle with salt, and brush the edges of the dough with egg wash. Bake for about 20 minutes, or until the puff pastry is golden and puffed. Top with basil and more za'atar. Seize the moment and enjoy at once.

Note: *To make the pesto, blend ½ cup (15 g) of fresh basil, 1 large clove of garlic, 2 tablespoons (30 ml) of olive oil, 2 tablespoons (20 g) of pine nuts, 2 tablespoons (20 g) of grated parmesan, and ⅛ teaspoon of salt in a food processor until smooth.*

Sfincione

For the Dough

1 tbsp (12 g) instant yeast
1 cup (240 ml) lukewarm water
1 tbsp (21 g) honey
2 cups (250 g) all-purpose flour
3 tbsp (45 g) fine semolina
1 tsp fine sea salt
3 tbsp (45 ml) extra-virgin olive oil

For the Sauce

3 tbsp (45 ml) extra-virgin olive oil
1 large onion, finely sliced
2 large cloves garlic, finely minced
6 anchovy fillets, coarsely chopped
1⅔ cups (330 g) tomato passata
1 tbsp (21 g) honey
2 tsp (6 g) dried oregano
¼ tsp fine sea salt
Freshly ground black pepper
12 sun-dried tomatoes, coarsely chopped

For the Crumb Topping

⅓ cup (40 g) breadcrumbs
3 tbsp (45 ml) extra-virgin olive oil
¼ cup (15 g) grated pecorino cheese
1 tsp dried oregano

2 tbsp (30 ml) olive oil
12 pitted black olives

Ah sfincione . . . The name alone will inspire you to bake. If you like focaccia, you will love this pie, which is basically a rustic focaccia with layers of added flavor. This is another recipe from Sicily, and they say that it gets its name from the Arabic word sfinge, *meaning "sponge," hinting at the Middle Eastern influence in the region. Its use of semolina flour is particularly interesting. A small amount of it will contribute to the spongy and tender texture of this bread. I highly recommend making the sfincione dough with a sourdough starter. One of my dearest friends, Elaine Boddy, aka sourdough master extraordinaire, has the perfect recipe in her book,* Whole Grain Sourdough at Home.

For many, this is a Sicilian holiday pizza, and for good reason. It is perfect for crowds and delicious alongside olives, cheeses, and other small plates. Double the quantities of the ingredients and make this in a half sheet pan for large gatherings.

Place the yeast, water, and honey in a small bowl and stir together. Let it sit until the mixture foams up, about 5 minutes. Add the flour, semolina, and salt, and mix together to combine. Add the olive oil and rub it into the flour with your hands to make crumbs. Stir in the water and yeast mixture and then stir everything together with a wooden spoon for about 10 minutes. Alternatively, place the dough in the bowl of a stand mixture, and knead on low speed for about 8 minutes, or until the dough is smooth and elastic. It will be a very wet dough, which will result in a moist bread. Cover the dough with plastic wrap and let it sit in a warm place for 1½ to 2 hours.

For the sauce, heat a pan over medium heat, add the olive oil, and sauté the onion for 15 minutes, stirring often. Stir in the garlic and anchovies, and cook for another 3 minutes. Add the tomato passata, honey, oregano, salt, and pepper. Give everything a stir and simmer for 20 minutes on low heat. Stir in the sun-dried tomatoes and set aside.

Make a crumb topping by combining the breadcrumbs, olive oil, pecorino cheese, and dried oregano. Rub together with your fingers until well combined and set aside.

Grease a rimmed 13 × 9–inch (33 × 23–cm) quarter sheet pan with olive oil. Transfer the dough to the pan and flatten with the tips of your fingers, forming small wells throughout the dough. Keep flattening the dough until it covers the entire pan. It may resist a bit, so give it a few minutes to rest and shape it again. Cover the dough with plastic wrap and let it rest for another 20 minutes.

Meanwhile, preheat the oven to 400°F (200°C). Spread the prepared tomato sauce over the dough and then layer it with the breadcrumb mixture and olives. Bake for 40 to 45 minutes, or until the dough is baked with a crisp and golden bottom. Let the pie rest in the pan for about 5 minutes before sliding a spatula around the edges of the pie to loosen. Gently invert the sfincione onto another baking sheet and transfer it to a cooling rack. Serve with olives, cheeses, and cured meat. Enjoy the moment.

Whole Wheat Cheese and Thyme Hand Pies

Makes 26 pies

3 cups (390 g) whole wheat flour (see Note)

1 cup (125 g) white bread flour or all-purpose flour

1½ tsp (8 g) fine sea salt

½ cup (120 ml) extra-virgin olive oil, plus more for working and brushing the dough (see Tip)

½ cup (115 g) plain yogurt

1 large egg

Leaves of 30 sprigs wild thyme, chopped or ½ cup (10 g) fresh za'atar

1 tbsp (10 g) yeast

2 tsp (8 g) sugar

¾–1 cup (180–240 ml) warm water, divided

Filling

2 cups (240 g) mozzarella or Nabulsi cheese, finely chopped or crumbled

Leaves of 5 sprigs thyme

The whole wheat makes these pies incredibly tender, wholesome, and flavorful. The yogurt adds moisture and tanginess. And the wild thyme or za'atar, if you can find it, adds life and the taste of the Levant itself. I used store-bought thyme for this recipe, but it is worth seeking out wild thyme from local farmers.

Combine the whole wheat flour, bread flour, and salt in a mixing bowl. In a separate bowl, mix together the olive oil, yogurt, egg, and thyme leaves. Set it aside. Proof your yeast by combining the yeast, sugar, and ½ cup (120 ml) of warm water, about body temperature, in a small bowl or measuring pitcher and let it sit for 5 to 10 minutes, or until the mixture foams up. Stream the yeast and water mixture into the flour and mix with your hands until the ingredients are well combined. Add as much water as you can manage the dough with—it should be sticky but still kneadable. Knead it on a surface greased with olive oil until the dough is smooth and no longer sticky, 10 to 15 minutes. Place the dough in a large bowl greased with olive oil, cover with plastic wrap, and let it rise in a warm place for about 90 minutes.

Preheat the oven to 400°F (200°C).

Separate the dough into 2-tablespoon (30-ml)-sized balls, about the size of golf balls. Then, cover the dough with a clean towel and let it rest for another 20 minutes. Roll out each ball so that it is about ⅛ inch (3 mm) thick and 4½ to 5 inches (11 to 13 cm) wide. Place about 1 tablespoon (8 g) of cheese onto the center of each, sprinkle with a few thyme leaves, and fold the sides of the circle inward to make a triangle. Pinch at the edges to seal the pie completely. It will open slightly while baking.

Place the dough parcels onto a large baking sheet and brush with olive oil. Bake in batches for about 12 minutes, or until the bottoms of the breads are lightly golden.

Note: *All-purpose flour may be substituted for all of the whole wheat flour in this recipe. You may also lighten the amount of whole wheat by changing the proportions. For example: 2 cups (260 g) of whole wheat flour plus 2 cups (250 g) of all-purpose flour, or 1 cup (130 g) of whole wheat flour plus 3 cups (375 g) of all-purpose flour. Different flours call for different amounts of liquid, so use water gradually as you go along, aiming for the moistest dough that you can work with.*

Tip: *Use olive oil instead of extra flour throughout your time working with the dough to keep it moist.*

All Things Sweet

Sweets. This is where our childhood begins and hopefully never ends. When we indulge in the joys of sweet things, we are children again. Some of our strongest memories are associated with sugar. Every culture throughout the world has some sort of dessert that tastes like home to them. In the Mediterranean, ingredients such as semolina, sesame, aniseed, tahini, honey, dates, walnuts, pistachios, clotted cream, sweet cheese, olive oil, and the perfumed scents of orange and rose water are characteristic.

Many of the most celebratory moments in our lives involve some sort of sweet confection. From the Middle East to southern Europe, sugar is always present for special occasions. It is one of the few ingredients that is relevant across continents. Just think about the expression of bliss that results after a loved one relishes a sweet you have made. The priceless reaction makes the effort all the more worthwhile.

This was one of my favorite chapters to write, primarily because the flavors brought me so many feelings of nostalgia. I bake to go back in time and experience memories all over again. Floral-scented desserts, warm and sticky stuffed pastries, comforting spiced puddings, nougat, and dainty coffee table cookies are all parts of the colorful upbringing that taught me how to eat.

In this chapter, you will find many of my own interpretations of the ingredients that I grew up with and recipes that I was inspired to develop while living in the Mediterranean. My cakes are often made with local ingredients such as olive oil, carob, almonds, pumpkin, and dates. I never did this to make them healthier; I just truly love these flavors in sweets. I found that they add depth and uniqueness. You will also find traditional recipes such as churros and alfajores with some added twists. And lastly, there are simple everyday sweets, like the Dark Chocolate Lazy Cake (page 135), to satisfy our last-minute cravings.

Here's to making room for dessert.

Sobremesa

When we indulge in dessert, we do so for pleasure. Unlike eating a meal for sustenance, eating dessert is a treat. We make time for it. *Sobremesa* is a romantic Spanish term for this. It goes on to mean more than just the sweet enjoyed after a meal. Sobremesa also describes the intimate and serene moment that takes place after the meal has ended and just before dessert is served. The moment when everyone at the table sits, chats, and contemplates. Time stops anywhere from a couple of minutes to a few hours. The best sobremesa is the longest. And this can occur on any given day of the week. No one is rushing or worried about productivity. Everyone just sits around the table to relax, laugh, and enjoy the presence of each other. This focus on living in the moment is a ritual that truly replenishes the soul. *Olé!*

Watermelon, Rose, and Pistachio Cheesecake

Makes 10–12 slices

There is an Old World Sicilian treat known as gelo di melone or "watermelon pudding." It is made by simmering fresh watermelon juice, sugar, and starch to make a thick pudding. The treat is then served with pistachios and shaved chocolate. The recipe traces back to medieval times and resembles faludhaj, a medieval Middle Eastern watermelon pudding made with honey and starch. The idea inspired me to infuse the pudding with rose and layer it onto a decadent cheesecake with a pistachio crust. Trust me, it is much simpler than it seems. Think of this cheesecake as a dessert version of a Mediterranean watermelon and cheese salad, as contradictory as that may sound. Refer to A Note on Techniques (page 161) for explanations on the methods used for this cake.

For the Crust

1 cup (125 g) unsalted ground pistachios

½ cup (50 g) almond flour, or additional ground pistachios

¾ stick (74 g) unsalted butter, melted, plus more for greasing the pan

4 tbsp (60 g) light brown sugar

⅛ tsp salt

For the Filling

3 (8-oz [226-g]) packages cream cheese, softened

4 large eggs

1 large egg yolk

1¼ cups (250 g) granulated sugar

2 cups (400 g) sour cream

2 tsp (10 ml) fresh lemon juice

1 tsp rose water

1 tsp vanilla extract

1 tsp finely grated lemon zest

Preheat the oven to 325°F (160°C) and lightly grease a 9-inch (23-cm) springform pan with butter. Line the bottom with parchment paper and set aside.

To make the crust, add the ground pistachios, almond flour, melted butter, brown sugar, and salt to a bowl. Rub the ingredients together to ensure that all of the crumbs are coated in butter. Spread the mixture onto the bottom of your prepared pan and pat it down with the bottom of a cup to create an even layer. Then place the crust in the refrigerator while you prepare the filling.

Beat the cream cheese in the bowl of a stand mixer until smooth. Add the eggs and egg yolk, one at a time, and mix until smooth. Add the sugar and continue mixing for about 2 minutes, or until the ingredients are well combined. Scrape the bottom of the bowl and add the sour cream, lemon juice, rose water, vanilla, and lemon zest and mix once again until there are no more lumps in the batter. Pour the mixture into the prepared pan. Take two large sheets of aluminum foil and stack one on top of the other. Then place the pan onto the center of the foil and bring the edges up to the sides of the pan, wrapping its edges. This will prevent water from seeping into the cheesecake. Place the pan in a bain-marie or water bath to regulate the temperature of the cake. Bake for 85 to 90 minutes, or until set. The cheesecake should be firm, and the center should have just a slight jiggle.

Remove the cheesecake from the water bath and unwrap the aluminum foil. Let the cheesecake cool at room temperature for 45 minutes to 2 hours. Then refrigerate it for at least 7 hours or overnight.

(continued)

For the Topping

3 cups (600 ml) watermelon juice (see Note)

⅓–½ cup (80–100 g) granulated sugar, depending on the sweetness of the melon

½ cup (60 g) cornstarch

⅛ tsp ground cinnamon

1 tsp rose water

For Garnish

Dried rose petals

Fresh strawberries, halved, quartered, or diced

Pistachios, chopped or slivered

After the cheesecake has cooled for at least 7 hours, prepare the watermelon topping. Add the watermelon juice and sugar to a medium saucepan and stir together. In a small bowl, mix together the cornstarch and ¼ cup (60 ml) of the juice mixture from the pan. Pour the cornstarch mixture into the pot and stir together. Turn the heat to high and bring the mixture to a boil.

Once the mixture comes to a boil, continue to cook it while stirring continuously for another minute or two. The pudding should have thickened, and the sides should begin to come away from the pan. Mix in the cinnamon and rose water. Let it cool in the pot for about 5 minutes and then spread it over the cheesecake. Use a serrated spatula dipped in water to even out the surface. Let the cake cool in the refrigerator for another hour. Slide a knife or serrated spatula around the edges of the cheesecake to loosen it before removing it from the pan. Top with dried rose petals, strawberries, and pistachios. Keep chilled.

Note: *To make the watermelon juice, simply blend seedless watermelon in a food processor until smooth and strain it.*

Variation: *Substitute graham cracker crumbs for the pistachio and almond flours in this recipe to make this nut-free. For a topping variation, substitute the watermelon pudding for mango–passion fruit jam or dried or fresh apricot compote.*

Mini Lemon and Poppy Loaves with Raspberry and Rose Drizzle

Makes 8 loaves

For the Cakes

1½ cups (200 g) all-purpose flour

2 tsp (8 g) baking powder

¼ tsp fine sea salt

3 tsp (10 g) poppy seeds

1¼ cups (250 g) granulated sugar

½ cup (120 ml) vegetable oil, plus more for greasing the pans

2 large eggs

1 cup (215 g) plain yogurt

2 tbsp (10 g) lemon zest

2 tbsp (30 ml) lemon juice

1 tsp vanilla extract

For the Raspberry and Rose Drizzle

1 tbsp (14 g) butter, melted

2 tbsp (40 g) cream cheese, softened

1–2 tbsp (15–30 ml) lemon juice, divided

1 cup (125 g) confectioner's sugar, sifted

¼ tsp rose water

2 tsp (10 g) raspberry jam

If there is one sweet in this chapter that you will make for an afternoon tea, let it be this one. Not only do these mini cakes look lovely on display, the scents of lemon and rose will be sure to bring joy to your guests.

Preheat the oven to 350°F (180°C) and lightly grease eight mini loaf pans, or one pan with eight spaces for mini loaves, with vegetable oil or butter.

For the cakes, combine the flour, baking powder, salt, and poppy seeds in a medium bowl. Set aside.

Mix the sugar and vegetable oil in a bowl until smooth, for about 2 minutes. Add the eggs, one at a time, and continue to mix until they are well incorporated into the batter. Add the yogurt, lemon zest, lemon juice, and vanilla, and mix until smooth.

Using a baking spatula, fold the flour mixture into the wet batter until it is smooth and free of lumps. Spoon the batter evenly among the eight mini loaf pans, about ½ leveled cup (120 ml) in each pan.

Bake the cakes for 24 to 26 minutes, or until the tops are lightly golden. Remove the cakes from the oven as soon as a skewer inserted into the center of a cake comes out clean or with a few cake crumbs.

Meanwhile, prepare the drizzle. In a medium bowl, combine the butter and cream cheese until smooth. Add 1 tablespoon (15 ml) of lemon juice and the confectioner's sugar. Mix until creamy. Stir in the rose water and raspberry jam and mix to combine. Add another tablespoon (15 ml) of lemon juice if the mixture is too thick. Set aside.

(continued)

For the Simple Syrup
½ cup (100 g) granulated sugar
½ cup (120 ml) water
1 tsp lemon juice
½ tsp rose water

For Garnish
Dehydrated raspberries
Dried rose petals
Poppy seeds

Then, prepare the simple syrup. Combine the sugar, water, and lemon juice in a small saucepan and bring to simmer. Gently boil the mixture while stirring, until the sugar is fully dissolved, about 3 minutes. Remove from the heat and stir in the rose water.

Brush the cooled cakes with hot simple syrup. Then, once the surfaces of the cakes are cool to the touch, spoon a teaspoon of the raspberry drizzle onto their centers. Spread it slightly so that it falls down the edges of the cakes.

Decorate the cakes with dehydrated raspberries, dried rose petals, and poppy seeds.

Fig, Walnut, and Olive Oil Biscotti

Makes about 24 cookies

2 cups (250 g) all-purpose flour

½ tsp fine sea salt

1½ tsp (6 g) baking powder

½ tsp ground cinnamon

1 tsp aniseeds

2 large eggs

⅓ cup (80 ml) extra-virgin olive oil

½ cup (100 g) granulated sugar

¼ cup (50 g) packed light brown sugar

2 tsp (10 ml) vanilla extract

2 tsp (8 g) toasted sesame seeds

½ cup (120 g) dried figs, stems removed, diced

⅓ cup (50 g) walnuts, toasted, coarsely chopped

⅓ cup (50 g) pistachio nuts, plus more for sprinkling (optional)

½ cup (70 g) dark chocolate, 70% cocoa solids, chopped

1 large egg white mixed with a pinch of salt, for brushing

Melted chocolate (optional)

This is a delicious treat to enjoy alongside your morning coffee or tea. The biscotti is filled with chewy figs, sweet aniseed, and crunchy walnuts. The olive oil adds depth, without an overpowering flavor.

Add the flour, salt, baking powder, cinnamon, and aniseeds to a medium bowl and whisk together to combine. In a separate bowl, beat together the eggs for about 3 minutes, or until light and frothy. Add the olive oil, granulated sugar, brown sugar, and vanilla and mix well to combine. Add half of the flour mixture and, using a spatula or baking paddle, fold until the flour is no longer visible. Add the other half of the flour mixture along with the sesame seeds, figs, walnuts, pistachios, and chocolate. Fold the mixture together just until it forms a dough. It should still be sticky. Place two large sheets of plastic wrap on a kitchen surface, separate the dough in half, and place each piece of dough onto the center of each piece of plastic wrap. Loosely cover both pieces with plastic wrap. Shape each piece of dough into a roll. Gently flatten using the palms of your hand to form two logs that are roughly 10 x 3 inches (25 x 8 cm). Tightly wrap each log with plastic wrap and refrigerate for 30 minutes.

Preheat the oven to 350°F (180°C) and line a large baking sheet with parchment paper or a silicone baking mat. Unwrap each log of dough onto the pan, leaving a few inches of space in between the two. With floured hands, shape the dough one last time so that the logs are about ½ inch (1.3 cm) thick. Brush the surface of the dough with egg wash and bake for 25 to 30 minutes, or until golden. Be sure to rotate the pan halfway through baking. Let the loaves cool for 15 to 20 minutes to allow for cleaner cuts. Using a serrated knife, slice the loaves horizontally with a slight slant to make pieces that are ½ inch (1.3 cm) wide. Arrange the biscotti cut side down on the baking sheet and bake for a total of 15 to 20 more minutes, 7 to 10 minutes on each side. The biscotti should be lightly golden and crisp.

Place the biscotti on a wire rack to cool completely. Dip halfway in melted chocolate and sprinkle with crushed pistachios, if you like. Once the cookies are cool, transfer them to an airtight container. The flavor of biscotti develops overnight and is best after 2 days. The cookies will keep well for 2 to 3 weeks, but they never seem to last that long in my kitchen.

Variation: *Feel free to use any dried fruit of your choice in place of the fig. I often use dried apricot, dried cranberries, and dried cherries.*

Dark Chocolate Lazy Cake

Serves 4

10.5 oz (300 g) good-quality dark chocolate, 70% cocoa solids, finely chopped

5 tbsp (75 g) unsalted good-quality butter

⅔ cup (200 g) sweetened condensed milk

½ tsp ground espresso powder

1 cup (65 g) digestive or Maria cookies, broken into small pieces

½ cup (16 g) crispy rice cereal

½ cup (65 g) pistachios, coarsely chopped

½ cup (70 g) hazelnuts, toasted, coarsely chopped

⅛ tsp fine sea salt

Cocoa powder or confectioner's sugar, for topping

Lazy cake is a Levantine dessert with likely English origins, a remnant of colonial times. It is indeed the perfect lazy day sweet and pairs wonderfully with coffee or tea. In Italy, a similar concept is known as salame di cioccolato *or "chocolate salami." I have gone with the latter for shaping this chocolate bar. Feel free to use what you have in your pantry for the filling. This dessert is also delicious with sour dried pomegranate or candied orange peel if you can get your hands on either. The options are endless. I prefer to use digestive cookies, which you can find in the international section of many grocery stores, but Maria cookies, which are more widely available, will also do.*

Place a medium pot over medium-high heat and fill it halfway with boiling water. Place a glass, heatproof bowl over the pot, making sure the bottom is not touching the boiling water. Add the chopped chocolate and butter and stir together until melted. Remove the bowl from the heat and stir in the sweetened condensed milk and espresso powder. Stir in the crushed cookies, rice cereal, pistachios, hazelnuts, and salt, and leave to cool for 5 to 8 minutes. Place the mixture onto a large rectangular piece of plastic wrap and shape it into a log sized about 8 × 3 inches (20 × 8 cm). Let it cool in the refrigerator for at least 50 minutes. Then mold the log again to get the perfect shape. Put it back in the refrigerator to cool for at least 4 to 6 hours before serving. Leave it overnight to get the smoothest cuts. Dust the bar with cocoa powder, slice, serve, and enjoy slowly.

Note: *If any variation causes the chocolate to separate, beat it with a mixer for a few minutes until smooth.*

Flourless Dark Chocolate and Olive Oil Cake with Pistachio Cream

Makes 8 slices

For the Ricotta-Pistachio Cream

½ cup (125 g) ricotta, drained and patted dry

¼ cup (33 g) confectioner's sugar, sifted

¼ cup (60 ml) heavy cream, whipped

½ cup (56 g) ground pistachios

½ tsp vanilla

½ tsp rose water

For the Cake

5 large eggs, room temperature, separated

1 cup (200 g) granulated sugar, divided

½ cup (120 ml) extra-virgin olive oil

7 oz (200 g) good-quality dark chocolate, 70% cocoa solids, finely chopped

1 tsp vanilla extract

¼ tsp fine sea salt

4 tbsp (24 g) cocoa powder

½ tsp espresso powder

For the Strawberries

1 cup (150 g) strawberries, sliced

3 tbsp (45 g) sugar

½ tsp rose water

A version of this cake has been the most popular recipe on my blog for over 5 years now. It is delicious on its own or with a side of salted caramel ice cream. But I especially love this pistachio and ricotta cream with macerated strawberries. Give it a try if you are in the mood for a special treat. I also recommend doubling the espresso powder for more intensity. You may heighten the cake by using an 8-inch (20-cm) pan, but add a couple minutes of baking time to the original recipe. The cake will be done when a skewer inserted into the center comes out clean or with a few crumbs.

Place the ricotta and confectioner's sugar in a food processor and pulse until smooth. Fold in the whipped heavy cream, ground pistachios, vanilla, and rose water. Keep the cream refrigerated until you're ready to use it.

Preheat the oven to 350°F (180°C) and lightly grease a 9-inch (23-cm) cake pan with olive oil. Line the bottom with parchment paper and set aside.

For the cake, use a mixer to whip the egg whites with ½ cup (100 g) of the sugar until stiff peaks form. Set aside.

Heat the olive oil in a small saucepan over low heat. Stir in the chocolate and quickly remove the pot from the heat. Stir the mixture until the chocolate is completely melted and smooth. Let it cool for about 3 minutes and spoon the chocolate into a mixing bowl.

Add the remaining ½ cup (100 g) of sugar to the chocolate mixture and whisk well. Then mix in the egg yolks, one at a time, until well incorporated into the batter. Add the vanilla and mix again. Combine the salt, cocoa powder, and espresso powder, and fold them into the batter. Lastly, fold in the whipped egg whites until the chocolate is dark and smooth.

Spoon the cake batter into the prepared pan and bake in a preheated oven for 22 to 25 minutes, or just until the center of the cake springs back when you touch it. A knife inserted into the center of the cake should come out with a few cake crumbs. Let the cake cool in the pan for at least 15 minutes before transferring to a wire rack to cool completely. Run a knife along the rim of the pan to loosen the cake.

In the meantime, combine the strawberries, sugar, and rose water in a bowl. Stir, cover, and refrigerate for 30 minutes before serving.

Serve the cake with a scoop of the ricotta cream and the macerated strawberries.

Spiced Pumpkin and Almond Cake with Dulce de Leche Cream

Serves 6

Autumn is such an inspiring season. Just when we are getting accustomed to the old, it all begins to fade away to make way for the new. New colors, new temperatures, and new harvests. The result of the changes are moments of revelation, such as the flavors in this cake. A version of it was one of my first blog posts several years ago when I began living in the Mediterranean. I was so inspired by the happy convergence of the pumpkin, almond, and olive harvests in October. Having reaped fresh, green spicy olive oil from the harvest, I thought that the flavor would complement the pumpkin divinely. The almond makes for an incredibly moist crumb. Here I have added a cajeta ganache and toasted almonds for the ultimate autumn comfort treat. Feel free to substitute dulce de leche for cajeta.

For the Cake

½ cup (120 ml) extra-virgin olive oil, plus more for greasing the pan

1 cup (115 g) packed fine almond flour, plus more for the pan

1 cup (125 g) all-purpose flour

½ tsp baking soda

½ tsp baking powder

¼ tsp fine sea salt

1 tsp ground cinnamon

¼ tsp ground nutmeg

¼ tsp ground cloves

¼ tsp ground allspice

½ cup (125 g) pumpkin puree

1 tsp vanilla extract

1 cup (200 g) granulated sugar

½ cup (100 g) light brown sugar

3 large eggs

For the Dulce de Leche Topping

½ cup (120 ml) heavy cream, whipped

⅔ cup (190 g) cajeta or dulce de leche

Pinch of sea salt

Pinch of ground cinnamon, plus more for topping

Almond slices, toasted, for topping

Preheat the oven to 350°F (180°C) and lightly grease the bottom and sides of a 9-inch (23-cm) springform pan with olive oil. Line the bottom of the pan with parchment paper and lightly flour its sides.

Add the almond flour, all-purpose flour, baking soda, baking powder, salt, cinnamon, nutmeg, cloves, and allspice to a bowl and mix well. In a separate bowl, combine the pumpkin puree, olive oil, vanilla, granulated sugar, and brown sugar. Mix until smooth and then whisk in the eggs, one at a time. Using a silicone baking paddle, fold the flour mixture into the pumpkin batter until the batter is smooth.

Spoon the cake batter into your prepared pan and bake for 35 to 38 minutes, or just until a skewer inserted into the center of the cake comes out clean. You know the cake is ready when it springs back when you gently poke its center. Let it cool for 10 minutes and gently slide a knife around its edges to loosen it. Invert the cake onto a cooling rack, gently remove the parchment paper, and let it cool completely.

For the topping, combine the whipped cream, cajeta, salt, and cinnamon. Fold the mixture using a baking paddle until it is well combined. Transfer the cake to a serving dish and top with the ganache, cinnamon, and toasted almonds.

Variation: *For a white chocolate ganache topping, heat ¼ cup (60 ml) of heavy cream in a small pot. Stir in 1 cup (170 g) of white chocolate chips and stir until smooth. Remove from the heat, stir in the sea salt, and drizzle the ganache over the cake.*

Cream of Rice Pudding with Apricot Compote

Serves 4

I grew up eating arroz con leche with my Latin family and roz bi haleeb with my Middle Eastern family. There are so many versions of rice and milk puddings throughout the world. One of the most popular desserts in Puerto Rico is tembleque, an ethereal coconut milk pudding thickened with rice flour or corn starch. In the Levant, mahalabia is a Levantine milk pudding infused with floral extracts and mastic. My version, which includes an orange blossom apricot compote, is a crossroads between the two worlds. It is also divine served simply with cinnamon and crushed nuts. Similar flavors can be found throughout North Africa in places such as Algeria and Tunisia.

2 tbsp (42 g) orange blossom honey

4 cups (960 ml) coconut milk or whole milk

½ cup (100 g) granulated sugar

⅛ tsp fine sea salt

½ cup (135 g) ground white rice flour

½ tsp rose water

½ tsp orange blossom water

Pistachios, for topping

Dried rose petals, for topping

For the Compote

5 medium dried apricots, chopped

¼ cup (50 g) granulated sugar

¼ cup (60 ml) water

1 tsp lemon juice

Small pinch of saffron

¼ tsp orange blossom water

Take out four dessert bowls, 4 to 4½ inches (10 to 11 cm) in diameter. Drizzle a teaspoon of honey onto the bottom of each bowl. In a small pot, combine the coconut milk, sugar, salt, and rice flour. Mix until smooth and bring the heat to medium-high. Simmer the milk mixture for 5 to 7 minutes, stirring often until it has a pudding consistency. Stir in the rose and orange blossom waters. Spoon the pudding into the prepared bowls. Drizzle another teaspoon of honey over the top of each bowl. Let the puddings sit out for 1 hour and then refrigerate them for at least 4 hours before serving.

To make the compote, add the dried apricots, sugar, water, lemon juice, and saffron to a saucepan. Stir together to combine and simmer the sauce for 5 to 8 minutes, or until it has the consistency of a light syrup. Remove the pan from the heat, stir in the orange blossom water, and set aside until serving.

Invert the dessert bowls onto serving dishes. Top the dessert with fruit compote, pistachios, and dried rose petals.

Variations: *Here are some topping ideas to play with that work wonderfully with the coconut: Mango and cardamom. Mango and passion fruit.*

Saffron Churros with Floral and Orange Syrup

Makes 15–20 churros

Versions of sweet fritters are popular around the world. There are all kinds of variations for fried dough served with some sort of sweet syrup or sugary coating. Nocatole and zeppola in Italy, churros in Spain and Latin America, and halabi and zalabia in the Levant and North Africa are just a few examples. They remind us of our childhood, summer nights, and festive occasions. In this version, I infuse the churros with saffron and soak them with a fragrant honey, orange, and floral syrup. The result is flavorful churros that are crispy yet moist. Each bite bursts with sweet syrup and will leave you wanting more.

For the Syrup

½ cup (120 ml) freshly squeezed orange juice

1 cup (200 g) granulated sugar

⅔ cup (160 ml) water

½ tsp orange blossom water

3 tbsp (60 g) orange blossom honey, optional

For the Churros

Sunflower or canola oil, for frying

Pinch of saffron (about 20 threads), soaked in 1 tbsp (15 ml) hot milk

½ cup (120 ml) whole milk

½ cup (120 ml) water

5 tbsp (75 g) butter, cut into cubes

2 tbsp (30 g) granulated sugar

½ tsp fine sea salt

1 cup (125 g) all-purpose flour

2 large eggs

½ tsp pure vanilla extract

To make the syrup, place a small saucepan over medium-high heat and add the orange juice, sugar, and water. Simmer the ingredients for 3 to 5 minutes, or until the liquid resembles a light syrup. Stir in the orange blossom water and honey, if desired. Set aside until serving the churros.

For the churros, heat about 2 inches (5 cm) of oil in a medium, heavy-based pot. Keep the temperature at 360 to 370°F (180 to 190°C).

In another pot, add the saffron-infused milk, whole milk, water, butter, sugar, and salt. Stir together, turn the heat to medium-low and bring to a simmer. Add the flour and stir the mixture continuously until smooth, for about 2 minutes. Remove the batter from the heat and spoon it into a mixing bowl. Add the eggs and vanilla and beat using an electric mixer until smooth.

Spoon the batter into a piping bag or dessert decorator fitted with a star attachment. I prefer to use the latter as it is firmer. Pipe the batter into the hot oil, in 6-inch (15-cm) pieces. Cut the ends with scissors.

Fry until golden brown, about 2 minutes per side. Place the churros on paper towels. Serve with orange and honey syrup right away.

> **Spice Routes:** Saffron not only imparts a vibrant golden hue to the dough, but a subtle floral taste as well. It marries beautifully with citrusy flavors and perfumes such as orange blossom water.

Alfajores with Cajeta

Makes about 18 cookie sandwiches

Tea and cookies with an oriental feeling. Conversations among people and places. Guitar playing and joy in the air. Treats resembling these were believed to have been served in the royal palaces of Al-Andalus during the Middle Ages. Alfajor does after all, come from the Arabic word meaning "luxurious," and I would not use any other word to describe it. The delicate, melt-in-your-mouth cookies are simply irresistible. In Latin America, a dulce de leche or cajeta filling is common. Cajeta is a goat's milk version of dulce de leche with a touch of cinnamon. If you have the time, I recommend my homemade fig filling.

1 cup (140 g) cornstarch or rice flour

½ cup (60 g) all-purpose flour

½ cup (40 g) fine dried desiccated coconut, plus more for rolling the cookies

½ tsp baking powder

¼ tsp fine sea salt

⅔ cup (80 g) confectioner's sugar, plus more for dusting

8 tbsp (113 g) unsalted butter, cold

2 large egg yolks, cold

1 tsp vanilla extract

For the Filling

1 cup (250 g) cajeta, dulce de leche, or fig paste

For the Fig Paste

7 medium dried figs, stems removed

2 tbsp (28 g) unsalted butter, melted

2 tbsp (42 g) honey

¼ tsp ground cinnamon

Pinch of fine sea salt

3 tbsp (45 ml) water

Preheat the oven to 350°F (180°C) and line a large baking sheet with parchment paper.

Add the cornstarch, flour, coconut, baking powder, salt, and confectioner's sugar to a food processor. Pulse the mixture until fine. Add the butter and pulse again until the mixture resembles a coarse meal. Add the yolks and vanilla and pulse one last time until the mixture comes together. Mold the dough into a ball, cover with plastic wrap, and let it chill in the refrigerator for an hour or overnight.

Remove the dough from the refrigerator and place it in between two pieces of parchment paper. As soon as it is malleable enough to work with, roll it so that it is ¼ inch (6 mm) thick. Cut the dough using a round, 2-inch (5-cm) ridged cookie cutter. Place the circles of dough onto the baking sheet, at least 1 inch (2.5 cm) apart.

Chill the dough in the freezer for 10 minutes before baking. This will ensure that the cookies keep their shape and do not spread while baking.

Bake the cookies until the edges are lightly golden, 10 to 12 minutes. Place them on a baking rack to cool.

To make the fig paste, let the dried figs soak in a bowl of water for 1 hour. Then drain and add the figs, butter, honey, cinnamon, salt, and water to a food processor. Pulse the mixture until smooth and set aside until ready to use.

Spoon 1 teaspoon of the filling onto the center of each cookie. Gently place one cookie filling side down onto another cookie to create a sandwich, and repeat until all the cookies are paired in sandwiches. Top with confectioner's sugar.

Note: *The cookies will keep for about 3 days in an airtight container.*

Date and Pecan Cake with Cream Cheese Frosting

Serves 6

This cake is a teatime favorite in my home. Chewy dates, crunchy pecans, and a decadent cream cheese frosting make this treat hit all of the spots. The warming scents of warm spices and toasted nuts make it perfect for the chillier parts of the year.

2 cups (250 g) all-purpose flour, plus more for the pans

2 tsp (8 g) baking powder

½ tsp fine sea salt

1 tsp ground cinnamon

¼ tsp ground nutmeg

1 cup (240 ml) vegetable oil

1½ cups (300 g) granulated sugar

½ cup (100 g) light brown sugar

1½ tsp (8 ml) vanilla extract

4 large eggs

1 cup (240 ml) whole milk

3 tbsp (50 g) sour cream or yogurt

1 cup (160 g) Medjoul dates, pitted and chopped, plus more for topping

⅔ cup (100 g) pecans or walnuts, toasted and coarsely chopped, plus more for topping

1–2 tbsp (21–42 g) date molasses, for topping

For the Cream Cheese Frosting

8 oz (230 g) cream cheese, slightly softened

1 stick (113 g) unsalted butter, slightly softened

2 cups (260 g) confectioner's sugar, sifted

Pinch of fine sea salt

½ tsp ground cinnamon

1 tsp vanilla extract

Milk, as needed

Preheat the oven to 350°F (180°C) and lightly grease and flour two 8-inch (20-cm) baking pans. Line the bottoms of the pans with parchment paper and set aside.

Add the flour, baking powder, salt, cinnamon, and nutmeg to a bowl and mix together. In a separate, large mixing bowl, beat together the oil, granulated sugar, brown sugar, and vanilla for about 2 minutes, or until light and creamy. Add the eggs, one at a time, and mix until smooth, another 2 minutes. Stir in the milk and yogurt. Then stir in the flour in two batches, just until the batter is smooth. Stir in the dates and toasted pecan pieces and spoon the batter into the prepared cake pans. Bake for about 40 minutes, or just until the center of the cake springs back after you gently poke it. A toothpick inserted into the center should come out clean or with just a few crumbs. Keep your eye on the oven for the last minutes of baking time so that the sponge does not overbake.

Invert the cakes onto a cooling rack and remove the parchment lining.

To prepare the frosting, mix the cream cheese until it is completely smooth and free of lumps. Add the butter and continue to blend until light and fluffy. Add the confectioner's sugar ⅓ cup (43 g) at a time and blend until smooth. Add the salt, cinnamon, and vanilla, and mix one last time to combine. If the frosting seems too thick, add 1 teaspoon of milk at a time until you get a creamy consistency.

Trim off the tops of the cakes, for evenness, if you like. Invert a cake onto a large serving dish and spread a third of the cream cheese frosting on top. Layer the other cake, cut side down, on top and spoon the rest of the frosting over the top. Spread it as decoratively as you like and top the cake with toasted nuts, date molasses, and chopped date pieces if you fancy.

Double Carob Brownies

Makes 9 brownies

⅔ cup (80 g) roasted carob powder, plus more for topping

½ tsp espresso powder

½ tsp fine sea salt, plus more for topping

½ cup (50 g) almond flour

½ cup (120 ml) extra-virgin olive oil

3 large eggs

⅓ cup (106 g) carob molasses

⅔ cup (133 g) granulated sugar

¼ cup (50 g) light brown sugar

1 tsp vanilla extract

⅔ cup (100 g) walnuts, toasted and chopped

These carob brownies are deep and decadent. They are as intense as brownies can possibly get. And they get this quality, surprisingly, without any chocolate at all. Carob comes from dried roasted pods that grow on carob trees throughout the Mediterranean. It has been harvested for thousands of years and is naturally sweet and immensely "chocolatey." Having grown up drinking traditional Levantine carob-infused beverages such as kharoub, I have a natural appreciation for the fruit. The use of carob and olive oil are not meant to replace chocolate and butter. The flavors are in a league of their own and deserve to be celebrated.

Preheat the oven to 350°F (180°C) and line the bottom and sides of an 8 × 8 inch (20 × 20 cm) pan with aluminum foil. Lightly spray the foil with cooking spray if you have it on hand.

Add the carob powder, espresso powder, sea salt, and almond flour to a medium bowl and mix to combine.

In another bowl, combine the olive oil and eggs and beat them on medium speed until light and frothy, about 4 minutes. Then add the carob molasses, granulated sugar, brown sugar, and vanilla and mix for another minute.

Add the carob and almond flour mixture to the batter and fold just until well incorporated. Stir in the nuts and scrape the batter into the baking pan. Bake for 28 to 30 minutes—the center should still be slightly fudgy and will harden as the brownies cool.

Cool the brownies for 20 minutes before cutting. Sprinkle with carob powder and sea salt, and enjoy at once!

Black Sesame Horchata

Serves 2

1 cup (160 g) toasted black sesame seeds

3 cups (720 ml) water

3 tbsp (60 g) honey, sugar, or sweetener of choice (see Note)

2 tbsp (32 g) tahini

1 tsp ground cinnamon

Pinch of fine sea salt

Splash of milk or milk alternative of choice, optional

I grew up drinking sesame horchata during my childhood summers in Puerto Rico. I found it to be one of the most refreshing beverages that one could enjoy on a scorching summer day. Variations of horchata exist throughout the Latin world. In Mexico, rice is most often used. In Puerto Rico, it is made from toasted sesame seeds. A combination of jicaro seeds and nuts are used in Central America. And in Spain, the birthplace of the delicious beverage, horchata is made with tiger nuts or chufa. My version makes use of both black sesame seeds and tahini. The black sesame adds color and depth and the tahini, a rich creaminess. A match made in heaven.

Place the sesame seeds in a small bowl and cover them with about 2 inches (5 cm) of water. Let the seeds soak overnight, and drain and rinse them the next day.

Transfer the sesame seeds to a blender. Add the water and honey and blend for 3 minutes, or until the liquid is completely smooth. Place two pieces of cheesecloth over a strainer fixed over a bowl. Add the sesame mixture and squeeze out the milk. Discard the pulp.

Rinse out the blender and pour the sesame liquid back inside along with the tahini, cinnamon, and salt. Blend it until well combined. Then strain the horchata twice and serve with a splash of milk if desired. You may double this recipe and refrigerate it. The beverage keeps well chilled for up to 4 days.

Note: *The horchata may also be sweetened with pitted and peeled dates.*

Winter Citrus Fruit Salad

Serves 2

2 tsp (11 g) pomegranate molasses

2 tbsp (30 ml) fresh lemon juice

1 tbsp (15 ml) extra-virgin olive oil

2 tsp (10 g) orange blossom honey

¼ tsp orange blossom water

½ pomelo, peeled and segmented

3 clementines, peeled and segmented

2 oranges, peeled and segmented

2 red grapefruits, peeled and segmented

1 cup (160 g) pomegranate arils

½ cup (20 g) fresh mint leaves

2 tbsp (20 g) almond flakes

1 tsp poppy seeds

The scent of citrus has the ability to fill us with joy and life on a dull winter's morning. It awakens our senses and makes everything better. I make this fruit salad for that simple reason. It also happens to be absolutely delicious, thanks in part to the unique flavor of pomelo. Pomelo is abundant and bursting with flavor in the Levant during the colder months of the year, and it is at its prime from December to February. Its flavor is similar to a sweet grapefruit but without any bitterness or sourness. Look for it at your local health foods store or at an Asian grocery.

Add the pomegranate molasses, lemon juice, olive oil, honey, and orange blossom water to a small bowl and mix together.

In a serving bowl, add the segmented pomelo, clementine, oranges, and grapefruits and toss the fruit together. Add the pomegranate, mint, almond flakes, poppy seeds, and the sweet pomegranate dressing and toss to combine. Enjoy right away.

A Note on Ingredients

You may get overwhelmed by seeing a long list of ingredients in a couple of the recipes in this book. But when you look closely, you will notice that they consist mostly of spices, herbs, and aromatics. Spices and aromatics can be purchased fresh once and kept in your pantry for a few months. I recommend buying small pots of herbs and keeping them inside or letting the herbs spread in your garden. Basic herbs such as mint, basil, oregano, chives, thyme, and parsley require little maintenance and can even flourish indoors. If they appear wilted, place them in a cup or bowl filled with water for 1 to 2 hours. This should bring them back to life.

The following are some not-so-obvious ingredients that are always in my kitchen pantry. Fortunately, they are also becoming more and more accessible throughout the world. Products such as freekeh, bulgur wheat, za'atar, and floral waters can now be found in many natural food stores. Also check with your local international or Middle Eastern food stores. If there isn't an ethnic food store in your locality, rest assured that you can find these ingredients online from the comfort of your own home. Adding new staples to your pantry will add new dimensions of flavor to your cooking.

A general note on ingredients: In this book, olive oil is always extra-virgin. Salt is fine sea salt or occasionally flaky or coarse for sprinkling over dishes. Parsley is always flat leaf. Eggs are always large.

Pantry Staples

Anchovies

Anchovies are small fish native to the Mediterranean. They add saltiness and a savory flavor to foods. Their fishy quality is only noticed if you add too much. A small amount in a recipe, however, will add depth, flavor, roundness, and natural salt. Use jarred anchovies to lift salad dressings, dips, bread toppings, stews, sauces, etc.

Bulgur Wheat

Bulgur is a grain made from dry, cracked wheat. It comes in a few varieties: fine, medium, coarse, and whole. Aside from the classic golden version, it also comes in a red-brown variation. Its flavor is nuttier and slightly more intense. I love it served with fall produce. Both varieties are great for pilafs, stews, and salads.

Carob

Carob is harvested from the carob tree. Its pods contain pulp that is harvested, roasted, and ground into a powder or made into molasses. I keep both roasted carob powder and carob molasses in my pantry. You can find it in the sauce in my Fried Eggplant with Carob-Maple Sauce recipe (page 32) and in the Double Carob Brownies recipe (page 148). Its flavor is deep, sweet, and chocolate-like with an added tang.

Farro

Farro is an ancient grain as old as time. Its flavor profile is nutty, slightly chewy, and robust. The grain's mild taste makes it work alongside most produce and meat dishes. Farro is the perfect complement to mushrooms (see my farro and mushroom pilaf on page 113). Like freekeh, it will keep its texture after being cooked. Adjust the cooking time as needed, as farro comes in different sizes.

Freekeh

Freekeh is an ancient grain native to the Fertile Crescent. Green durum wheat is harvested while young and roasted over an open fire. This process contributes to its deep, smoky, and nutty flavor. Freekeh is hearty, satisfying, and forgiving to cook. It comes in four main varieties: fine, medium, coarse, or whole. In the West, the medium and coarse versions are most common. I grew up eating it in stews, but I love it cooked as a risotto, as a pilaf, or in warm salads.

Harissa

This North African chili sauce is essential to the cuisines of Tunisia, Morocco, and Algeria. It is made with roasted red pepper, chili pepper, garlic, lemon, and spices. Harissa's flavor profile is spicy, smoky, and garlicky. The paste is delicious alongside meats, fish, and seafood, as in the Mediterranean White Fish with Herb Sauce (page 72).

Jarred Roasted Red Pepper

Having a jar of roasted red pepper around is useful for quickly adding smokiness to dishes. It lifts the Artichoke and Cannellini Paella (page 102), adding another level of flavor. It is also delicious in dips and sauces.

Preserved Lemon

Preserved lemons are an indispensable condiment in the kitchen. They have a tart, tangy, salty, and fermented quality that makes dishes sing. Their complexity and depth cannot be replaced with regular lemons. They are my definition of gusto! Lemons are preserved in the winter while they are at their peak. The use of preserved lemon is common in North African countries such as Egypt, Morocco, Algeria, and Tunisia. It can be used for many dishes that call for lemon zest. I love using preserved lemons to bring roasts, dips, and sauces to new depths.

To make, prepare a large, sterilized jar and fill it with 8 to 10 unwaxed lemons that have been cut into wedges. Sprinkle 2 tablespoons (30 g) of salt over each layer—you will use about ½ cup (100 g) total. Push the lemons down to release their natural juice. If you need to add more liquid to cover the lemons, pour lemon juice over the top. Push down the lemons every few days and skim off any white foam that forms. Preserve them for at least 4 weeks. The longer they sit, the more the flavors will develop. Rinse well before using to remove any excess salt. Use the skin and rind and discard the pulp when you cook.

You can also infuse preserved lemons with spices and herbs such as cinnamon sticks, cloves, thyme, rosemary, bay leaves, or chili.

Orange Blossom Water

Orange blossom or azahar derives from the Arabic *azaahir*. Popular in both Spanish and Middle Eastern traditions, the flowers that sprout from the orange trees have been historically known for their beautiful fragrance, flavor, and therapeutic properties. The scent is most often used for infusing sweet syrups and desserts. However, a dash also works divinely in dishes such as the basmati pilaf (page 117). Orange blossom water complements orange fruits such as oranges, clementines, apricots, and peaches.

Pomegranate Molasses

Pomegranate molasses is made by reducing fresh pomegranate juice to a sweet, tart, and sour syrup. It is delicious in salad dressings, sauces, or meats. I usually buy pomegranate molasses from Lebanese or Turkish makers, who are quite skilled at making it.

Rose Water

Rose water is used in the same way as orange blossom water. It works particularly well with red fruits such as strawberries, cherries, pomegranates, and raspberries. It is perfect for infusing syrups and compotes.

Shatta or Sweet Chili Sauce

Shatta is a sweet chili sauce used in Palestinian, Lebanese, and Syrian cuisines. It is usually made with red chili, garlic, lemon, salt, and a bit of sugar. I love using it with ground meat or vegetable dishes. Not all versions are sweet, and some are spicier than others. Taste a few varieties and use what you like.

Tahini

Tahini has become commonplace now and can be found in grocery chains throughout the West. I use it in hummus, sauces, beverages, and alongside meat and fish dishes. The paste adds both creaminess and nuttiness to recipes. I often use it to add weight to lighter dishes. I favor Lebanese and Nabulsi varieties, which are mild, thick, rich, and creamy.

Tamarind

Tamarind is derived from the Arabic word *tamar hindi*, meaning "Indian date." The fruit, which is extracted from the pods of the tamarind tree, is sweet, tangy, and sour. You will often find the concentrated pulp sold in ethnic food stores, but I recommend getting the paste, which is ready to use. It can be easily found online. Tamarind is quite popular in Levantine cuisines, particularly for meat dishes such as traditional stuffed carrots in tamarind sauce. I like to use it in the Braised Lamb Shanks with Tamarind (page 53) and Sweet and Sour Tamarind Shrimp (page 86). A little goes a long way and will impart sweet, sour, and bitter flavors to your food.

Spices

Spices always taste better when they are fresh. Look for spices that have not been on the shelves for too long, preferably from South Asian or Middle Eastern grocers. Buy whole spices in small amounts, toast them in a dry pan until aromatic, crush or grind them, and use over the course of a few months. On more relaxed cooking days, I recommend toasting and crushing the spices by hand just before using them. Toasting spices, like nuts, brings out their natural oils, flavors, and aromas. Not only will your food taste better, but cooking will also be more pleasurable.

The texture that results from using a mortar and pestle is also different than when using a food processor. Sauces will be creamier and spice and nut mixes more powdery or paste-like. If you are grinding large batches, use a machine. But when making small meals or on more relaxed cooking days, you will notice a difference when using a mortar and pestle. Not only will your food be more delicious, but the cooking experience will be more pleasurable. In the past, everything was pounded. And if you seek to discover the best hummus joints, you will find that they still pound massive batches of garbanzos by hand.

Aleppo Chili Flakes

Aleppo chili or Halaby pepper is a chili variety that originated in Aleppo, Syria. It is widely popular in Levantine and Turkish cuisine and its flavor can be characterized as rich, deep, and sweet. Aleppo chili's mildness is what I most appreciate, allowing for intense chili flavor without the added heat.

Allspice

Allspice is used to add warmth to dishes, and it is usually combined with other deep spices such as cinnamon and nutmeg. It is common in eastern Mediterranean cuisine and is usually part of spice mixes such as 7 spice. Use the whole berry for flavoring stocks and pilafs and the ground spice for rubs or sweets.

Anise

Anise is similar to fennel, and both have a licorice flavor. Anise, however, is mild and sweet and goes well with sweets like these fig and nut biscotti (page 132).

Black Pepper

Black pepper has always been known as the king of spices. However, it is often only lightly sprinkled into a dish. Recipes usually combine salt and pepper in one line, but each condiment is in a league of its own. Black pepper is strong, aromatic, and of course, peppery. Use it generously and taste the difference in your food. Freshly grind it in the moment, as it becomes flat with time.

Cardamom

Cardamom pods impart a fresh, aromatic, and floral quality to dishes. The spice almost acts to "cleanse" meats and poultry, particularly lamb. It is delicious in the Braised Lamb Shanks with Tamarind (page 53). Ground cardamom is best for rubs, while the pods are great for infusing sauces, pilafs, stews, and milk-based desserts.

Cinnamon

Fragrant cinnamon is used for infusing pilafs, stews, braises, and pickled foods. Its woody and sweet flavor is delicious in this fish and seafood fideuá (page 81). Use the whole sticks for infusions, and the ground spice for rubs and baking. Look for Ceylon cinnamon, which is more delicate than cassia.

Coriander

Coriander is essential to Mediterranean cooking. It is warm, sharp, and slightly citrusy. Use it in dishes that ask for cilantro for an added layer of flavor. Use the whole spice for marinades like the one used in the roasted chicken with lemon and dates (page 58). The ground spice is great for rubs, especially for seasoning fish.

Cumin

Cumin is earthy, rich, and bittersweet. This flavor profile works well with legume-based dishes and dips. It also aids with digestion. The whole seeds are divine toasted and tossed with a warm pilaf like this basmati and herb pilaf (page 117) for little punches of flavor.

Dukkah

Dukkah is an ancient Egyptian spice mix containing a variety of spices, nuts, and seeds. It adds toasty and earthy notes to a variety of dishes, especially roasted vegetables like this Roasted Cauliflower and Eggplant with Dukkah and Chili (page 97). The usual suspects are hazelnuts, sesame seeds, coriander, and cumin seeds. But you can play around with the flavors and use other nuts and spices such as pistachios, walnuts, and dried herbs. Be sure to toast the nuts, spices, and seeds to really bring out their flavor.

To make a basic dukkah, combine ½ cup (65 g) of toasted hazelnuts, ⅓ cup (54 g) of toasted sesame seeds, 1 tablespoon (6 g) of toasted coriander seeds, and 1 tablespoon (8 g) of toasted cumin seeds in a mortar. Pound the mixture until it is mostly ground and generously season with salt and pepper. Sprinkle over dips, soups, roasted vegetables, and salads.

Fennel

Fennel seeds are native to the Mediterranean and are characterized by a sweet and savory licorice flavor. The spice complements meats, poultry, sauces, and breads. The seeds are sometimes used in dukkah and 7 spice to add sweet and pungent notes.

Pimentón Dulce

Pimentón originated in Spain. It was the result of the discovery of red peppers in the New World. The creation of the spice gave the Spanish some autonomy from depending on other empires for spices. Over time, it became the most important spice in some of Spain's most iconic dishes, such as paella.

Pimentón can be used interchangeably with sweet or smoked paprika. However, pimentón dulce ahumado, or smoked pimentón dulce, is sweeter and smokier. Its unique flavor is the result of a centuries-old process that calls for drying the capsicum peppers and smoking them over oak wood. I use pimentón dulce in most recipes, such as the Artichoke and Cannellini Paella (page 102) or the seafood and fish stew (page 68). Look for the vintage-looking tins from Spain.

Saffron

Saffron, or azafrán, as it is known in Spain, is warm, aromatic, and floral. It imparts beautiful, deep, golden hues to dishes such as the basmati pilaf (page 117) or these Saffron Churros with Floral and Orange Syrup (page 143). I always soak a pinch (about 20 threads) in a small bowl of hot milk or water for at least 10 minutes to get the most flavor out of it. Look for Iranian or Spanish saffron, which are the best varieties.

Sesame

I have three varieties of sesame in my kitchen: raw, toasted, and toasted black. I use the raw seeds when they are going to be exposed to heat in recipes such as the halloumi with honey sauce (page 36) and seeded chicken breasts (page 62). Black sesame is slightly deeper and nuttier in flavor. Try it in the Black Sesame Horchata (page 151). Be careful not to confuse black sesame with the sharp nigella, or black cumin seed, which can be quite bitter in large amounts.

7 spice

7 spice is a fragrant Levantine spice mixture that consists of allspice, cinnamon, coriander, black pepper, cumin, cloves, and white pepper. Some versions also have turmeric and ginger. The spice combination is mostly used for meat and rice dishes, but adding it to vegetables will embolden them.

Sumac

Sumac, which is native to the Mediterranean, is made from grinding sumac berries. Some varieties and potential substitutes exist in the States, such as staghorn sumac and smooth sumac. The spice imparts a vibrant and lemony tang to salads and marinades. It is especially divine in poultry dishes, like the Roasted Chicken with Pomegranate Glaze and Sumac (page 61) or Musakhan Salad (page 65). The spice can go rancid quickly, so keep large amounts in the freezer for best results.

Urfa Chili

Urfa is a Turkish chili variety with a smoky, mild, and rich flavor. I love adding it to the carob sauce in the eggplant fritters (page 32) for added intensity. Look for it in the Turkish section of an international food store or online.

Za'atar

Za'atar is an earthy eastern Mediterranean spice mix made with dried wild thyme, oregano, marjoram, sesame, and salt. Many versions contain sumac, which imparts a citrusy flavor and ruby color to the blend. Others are made with olive oil, which makes it darker and more moist. I prefer the simple mixture of herbs, sesame, and salt, which results in a bright green color and almost powdery texture. The blend is delicious as a topping for roasted vegetables, in soups such as the sweet potato and lentil soup (page 27), on dips and breads, and the list truly goes on and on.

A Note on Techniques

Bain-Marie

This technique ensures even heating in puddings, cheesecakes, flan, or other custards. It requires two pans: the pan that you will bake in and a larger plan to place it in. The larger plan is filled halfway with boiling water just before baking, preferably in the oven. If you are using a springform pan, it is best to wrap its exterior with aluminum foil to prevent water from seeping in.

Chilling Dough

Chilling cookie and pie doughs makes all of the difference in the final appearance and texture of your baked good. A shortbread cookie that has been chilled before baking will hold its shape much better than one that was left at room temperature.

Weighing

I never use a kitchen scale when cooking, but it is an absolute necessity during baking. It is useful for getting consistent results every time. Ingredients such as flour, for example, differ greatly depending on how lightly or tightly they are packed into measuring utensils.

Taking Temperature

A food thermometer is useful for keeping the temperature of oil consistent. This will ensure just the perfect golden color in your sweets. It is also convenient for preventing syrups from burning.

Testing Cake Doneness

Overbaking your cake by a few minutes can make all of the difference between a moist and a dry cake. During the last 6 minutes or so of baking time, I recommend gently poking the center of the cake. If it springs back, it is done. If not, add another few minutes of baking time and repeat. Visually, if a cake is ready, it will pull away from the sides of the pan. If something goes wrong and you overbake your cake, not all is lost. Brush some simple syrup over the top to add moisture.

Acknowledgments

I want to express my deepest gratitude to all of the lovely people who made this book possible. A very special thank you goes out to my publisher, Will Kiester, for believing in my work and supporting this project. I could not be any happier with the publishing house that I partnered with to deliver *Mediterranea*. This publication would not have been possible without my dear editor, Aïcha Martine Thiam, who chose to work with me and guided me from beginning to end. Her warmth, kindness, and attention to detail made this book a joy to write. Many thanks to Meg Baskis and Kylie Alexander for laying out these pages and designing a beautiful book. I would like to extend a special thanks to Hayley Gundlach, the managing editor at Page Street, for her final touches to the book and for bringing the publication into being. I am also grateful to Lee Rodman for her meticulous eye for detail and fine-tuning of this text.

Many thanks to all of the wonderful people who have supported me since I first began publishing stories and recipes on my blog, Hanady Kitchen. You gave me the courage to pursue this project further and continue sharing my narrative. Social media has made the world smaller, and I am grateful to have the opportunity to connect to my readers in such a personal manner. I would also like to extend a very special thank-you to my dear friend and longtime pen pal, Elaine Boddy. Not only is she immensely talented, but she is also one of the kindest and most selfless people that I know. I am also deeply grateful to the brilliant Aziz Abu Sarah for his support, feedback, and book endorsement.

I am deeply thankful to everyone else who made this happen, from my family and friends who assisted in tasting recipes, to the kind people who offered their feedback on visuals. I am grateful to my mother and father for their support. Additionally, I send a special thank-you to my mom, for helping me with my babies as I wrote and photographed this book. Many thanks to Yeli and Christine, for your loving friendships and support. And I send much gratitude to my cousin, Hoda, for simply being an amazing human being.

Every step that I have taken since my children were born has been for them. Salma and Ghaith, this book is for you. I am thankful for your existence and for having you both in my life. You taught me unconditional love, and you gave me the motivation to be the best version of myself. Thank you for being my inspiration always.

Last but not least in any way, I thank you, the owner of this book, for supporting this publication and the message of sharing plates, building bridges, and eating well along the way. I sincerely hope that you enjoy this book and the recipes it has to offer. And I look forward to connecting with you in the culinary adventures to come.

About the Author

Hanady is a Palestinian/Spanish American writer, photographer, recipe developer, and blogger. She is the founder of the website hanadykitchen.com, where she regularly posts recipes influenced by the flavors of her upbringing. Hanady is also a graduate of international affairs and has lived and traveled throughout the eastern Mediterranean. She has been nominated for a James Beard Foundation award and featured in *Food and Wine* and *Health*, among other publications. Hanady currently lives in Florida with her two children.

Index